PRAISE FOR SHIFT HAPP

To aspiring controllers: "Shift Happens" is your roadmap to navigating the complexities of modern finance roles. It provides invaluable insights into the challenges and opportunities facing accounting teams today, essential for those aiming to lead effectively. For CFOs, this book offers a clear-eyed perspective on enhancing financial operations and driving organizational success.

— Jerry Raphael, Veteran Accounting Leader and CFO

In today's fast-paced business environment, success depends on the ability to adapt, strategize, and innovate. "Shift Happens" illustrates how adopting an operational mindset in accounting and finance teams can empower this adaptability. Mike and Stefan's firsthand experience provides invaluable strategic advice for future leaders and current CFOs, offering fresh perspectives on optimizing financial operations and achieving business excellence.

— Roy Luo, General Partner at ICONIQ Growth

In "Shift Happens: The Rise of the Operational Mindset and How Controllers Can Drive Real Value," Mike Whitmire and Stefan van Duyvendijk offer a compelling exploration into the evolving role of controllers in today's dynamic business landscape. Drawing from their extensive industry experience and insights from finance leaders across top organizations, this book is a vital resource for anyone aspiring to excel in financial management and strategic leadership.

As someone deeply immersed in transforming Lovevery's accounting and finance functions amidst rapid growth, I understand firsthand the pivotal role of controllers in driving organizational success. "Shift Happens" delves into critical aspects often overlooked in traditional education, providing actionable strategies for enhancing leadership acumen and leveraging technology to streamline financial operations.

The authors' emphasis on the operational mindset resonates strongly with me, as it aligns with my approach at Lovevery, where we've harnessed technology to revolutionize transaction processing and enhance audit efficiencies. The book's insights on transaction automation and the integration of analytical tools for audits are particularly pertinent, reflecting the challenges and opportunities controllers face in today's digital age.

"Shift Happens" isn't just a book; it's a roadmap for navigating the complexities of modern finance roles with clarity and foresight. Whether you're aiming to deepen your strategic impact or refine your operational prowess, this book equips you with the knowledge and tools to thrive in the controller's seat. I wholeheartedly recommend it to anyone committed to advancing their career in finance.

— **Ashley Griesshammer, VP, Controller, Lovevery**

SHIFT HAPPENS

THE RISE OF THE OPERATIONAL MINDSET AND HOW CONTROLLERS CAN DRIVE REAL VALUE

MICHAEL WHITMIRE

STEFAN VAN DUYVENDIJK

FLOQAST BUSINESS PUBLISHING

ISBN: 979-8-218-41479-5 (Paperback edition)

Cover design and illustrations by The Vivere Design Team

MIKE

To Mom for inspiring me and Alison for supporting me

STEFAN

To my Mother and Grandmother, I wouldn't be who I am without their support

CONTENTS

FOREWORD

Over the last 20 years, I've learned that accounting and finance touch literally every part of an organization. This lesson has come through a combination of experience in different roles and working with a number of brilliant business leaders who understand — or learned to understand — the true value of accounting and finance, and are forward-thinking enough to try something new, even when conventional wisdom (of the time) might say different.

The accounting and finance world isn't just the numbers that appear in the financials, but rather all the groups and all the people in those groups across the organization. If we can be a better partner with those groups, we're going to help the company to achieve its goals and to get where we all want to get to.

Being that kind of partner to your organization is what the operational approach is all about.

I didn't have a label like "the operational approach" for what I was doing and for my team, but the ideas in this book resonate with me.

Today, as CFO of OnSolve, we've slowly built the baseline of an accounting and finance organization that strives to function as a partner for the business. We've done that through building great relationships with our dev teams, with the marketing organization, and with sales operations. We understand what drives our pipeline, so our bookings are better. Our forecasting is much better because our foundation in operations shows us what's really driving growth and retention.

The operational approach, as Mike and Stefan define it here, is the playbook for how to run not just a modern financial department — but a business. It's acting as an internal consultant, finding ways to maximize the efficiency of other parts of your organization and to help all those parts move together in synchrony to achieve its goals. You're always looking for ways to improve things in accounting and finance and across your organization. I kept my eyes on this approach as I moved up the ranks in accounting departments and as I moved into more strategic finance positions, and that has contributed to my success over the years, for which I am intensely grateful.

Beyond its business benefits, the operational approach is for all finance and accounting professionals: It's for accountants who want more than simply checking another box in an endless series of checklists. It's for accountants who have the mindset of being eager to learn and to bring value to the business in a better way. It's for finance professionals who aspire to reach the highest levels of leadership in their organizations, whether that's as CFO, CAO, or COO, as Stefan and Mike envision for the future. And it's also for those who are happy where they are, but also want to improve things in their section of the organization.

Technology and our systems are getting more sophisticated, and as a result, the accounting team and the financial planning team have more time to put together a much higher quality product every month. They're not just spitting out the numbers and immediately starting the cycle for the next month. The organization as a whole gets more insights into what's going on.

We have more time to establish relationships with others across the organization.

I'm not talking about just getting a coffee or an occasional lunch with someone in production or sales, but opening up the lines of communication and developing the mutual trust that leads to collaborating to make things easier and more efficient for everyone. With that foundation of trust, we can create something together that's better than we would have come up with on our own. These relationships can also make the job more fulfilling: pulling you away from the deadline-driven work of the monthly cycle and instead presenting an opportunity to work on something more interesting, more analytical, and ultimately, more rewarding and enjoyable.

If you fully embrace this approach, you get to do more than the flux analysis or the budget-to-actual comparisons, which are often positioned as the "more interesting" things that accountants get to do. You get to do the higher level analytical work that makes finance exciting. You can really get into the nuts and bolts of how the business works and learn about areas that you don't usually think about. You learn the details of how your organization produces what it sells. Your focus moves from getting your monthly work done to finding ways to improve things for everyone.

You will bring value to the business in a deeper way.

Here at OnSolve, because we have those collaborative relationships across the organization and because we're embedded into operations, people are coming to the accounting and finance teams for advice. Instead of hearing about complex deals after the fact, we are beginning to have a seat at the table when the deals are happening.

This is the fun part of the job that can be yours when you embrace the operational approach.

Throughout my career, I've been fortunate to have great mentors who have been instrumental in my learning and growth. I've also been fortunate to have been able to be a good mentor for others and to see people I've worked with get promoted into CFO roles. No one can have too many mentors, so whether you have powerful mentors in your current role or you're on your own, this book can mentor you.

This book is a playbook for shifting into a more operationally focused role. You will still have to go out and build those relationships, presenting yourself and your team as partners for the organization at large. And you will still have to do the monthly reporting and analysis.

But embracing the operational approach, as Mike and Stefan clearly explain here, can both help your company achieve its goals and bring more enjoyment and fun to your work, as well as unlimited opportunities to keep learning.

Bruce Duner, CFO, OnSolve

INTRODUCTION: OPERATIONAL ACCOUNTING IN REAL LIFE

We were on an optimization call with the controller of a global tech company, and we were looking at his actual FloQast instance. We noticed he was doing a lot more workflows than just the close process. It boggled Mike's mind because "I knew that he had other pieces of software that do those processes. He had workflows for SEC reporting and payroll and FP&A." So Mike asked him, "Dude, you have other tools for reporting. Why are you using FloQast for SEC reporting? That doesn't make any sense."

"I use those tools for the output, for the financial statements that are being produced," he responded. "But I need to know what they're doing, what their status is. So I have them log into FloQast so I can track their workflow and they can sign off in a central location. It helps me see what's going on throughout the month."

That was a big lightbulb moment for us. So, we went through our database to see if other clients had hacked FloQast for other operational-type workflows, and we found that around 30% were.

These CFOs and controllers were putting all those different operational functions under the office of the CFO into one workflow tool. They were seeing a lot of value in knowing what everyone was doing, how they were doing it, and when. They could understand how their teams collaborated with others across the organization. These controllers were taking their skills in optimizing and streamlining the accounting processes for closing the books, and bringing that to the broader organization.

If you don't have something that collects that information, you're flying blind, or trying to just trust your gut. As a recent McKinsey report[1] put it:

> *Too many companies still run their operations blindfolded. Limited information sharing and collaboration among functions, sites, and business units make optimal decision making slow and unwieldy — or impossible. And internal coordination is only a fraction of the challenge.*

Even in the office of the CFO, there are silos, which is what the controller of our tech company customer needed visibility into. As the old adage goes, "decisions are only as good as the underlying information," and controllers are tired of decisions being made with no information at all. With access to the analytics, the company's controller could see where the actual bottlenecks were. Which process is late every month? What causes downstream impacts? That helped him identify which processes to work on, to see if it can get done faster.

By operationalizing workflows, these controllers are redefining themselves. Instead of being relegated to the back office, as a cost center, as the people who say no, and who make everyone's jobs more difficult, these forward-thinking controllers are positioning themselves as the nerve center of the company.

The operational approach doesn't just make the accountants' jobs easier — it makes the whole enterprise function more efficiently.

As it already is, the controller oversees a bit of finance and reporting and a bit of tax in the workflows, and they're responsible for tracking the people around that. And so with that, they have really broad insight into the operations of the whole finance office.

And, as we'll explore in more detail in this book, accountants are the best ones to be catalysts of change and therefore the best ones to be in charge of operations. It's in our DNA to trust, but verify. We're used to having our work reviewed so we can grow and improve. Other parts of an organization don't have that tradition, so they can get stuck in staleness and confirmation bias. Due to the high-pressure environment accountants are raised in, it has become second nature for accountants to always be looking for better ways to do things, so when you put accountants in charge of operations, we bring that dynamic to the whole organization. Accountants also are the only part of a company (except maybe HR) that has contact with the entire organization.

Before we get too far, we want to make it clear that while having a tool like FloQast to monitor operations will make it easier to improve operations, the operational approach isn't about just strapping on a workflow tool, but still keeping your head down in the weeds of closing the books. Operational accounting is about taking a holistic view of the organization, and understanding that accounting is the guts of an organization.

Getting that information in one place is just one aspect of taking an operational approach to accounting. Accounting has always been about looking at the past. And, as companies grow and scale, having well-defined and well-documented processes is really important for consistency.

WE'RE ON THE OPERATIONAL TRACK WITH YOU

The idea for FloQast emerged out of co-founder Mike Whitmire's firsthand frustration. When he concluded a three-and-a-half-year stint as an auditor at EY to work as a revenue accountant at Cornerstone OnDemand, a SaaS startup, he was struck by the chaos of the month-end close. In his new job, Mike was constantly in Salesforce, checking on contracts so he could translate promises made by sales reps into the timing of revenue recognition.

> *And I realized Salesforce is a solution that is used by a team of individuals to help accomplish a collective goal, which is hitting a revenue target. The close is a team of individuals working towards a collective goal, which is a deadline-driven goal. And since it's a deadline that is non-negotiable, that's why we have to work a ton of hours to get it done. So Salesforce was much of the inspiration for FloQast. I wondered why accountants did not have their own version of Salesforce to solve our pain points around collaboration to manage the month-end close.*

So Mike, Chris Sluty, and Cullen Zandstra founded

FloQast in 2013 to fill the gap. FloQast was intended to simplify the workflow, checklists, and reconciliations, and to improve collaboration and efficiency around the month-end close. But, once we noticed that some of our customers – like the controller of that global tech company – were hacking FloQast to cover other workflows around the organization, we built a variation called FloQast Ops to make that easier.

After 11 years, FloQast has reached an inflection point as a business. We're going from all hands on deck trying to figure stuff out and get things done, to growing up as a business. We've grown from just the three founders doing everything to over 600 employees as of the end of 2023, and from a tiny office in a converted house to a global company with offices in Los Angeles, London, and Australia — not to mention just over $100 million in ARR.

We suddenly need to formalize our operations to eliminate our own pain points. Starting with this exact point in our history, this foundation we build now will be impactful for how well we succeed. So throughout this book, we'll share a few glimpses of what we're going through as we move down this path of operational accounting.

WE'RE NOT THE ONLY ONES ON THE OPERATIONAL TRACK

While stories from our clients like the one above inspire and delight us, we wanted data to confirm that what we were hearing was real, and not just anecdotal evidence from within our bubble of FloQast team members and customers. So in 2022 and 2023, we worked with the University of Georgia Consumer Analytics program as an independent research partner to take the pulse of accountants across the country. We had a strong suspicion of what was going on in the world of corporate accounting, but we wanted to validate what we were thinking and see if we could use those insights to help accountants have better lives.

It was crucial to us that our research partner was unbiased and wholly independent so that we could trust the data. Too often, so-called surveys are performed by pay-to-play entities and the results align neatly with the confirmation bias of the entity paying for the research. We wanted to make sure that we were seeing the true picture of what's out there, not what we were hoping to see. We published our findings as our Controller's Guidebook series, which is available on our website. We're including excerpts of this research throughout this book, and we hope you find it as illuminating as we did.

One of the most powerful insights to come out of this research is that many of the ideas we present in this book aren't just pie in the sky ideas; there are organizations that have achieved the elusive positive work/life balance, where team members have fulfilling careers, feel valued at work, are confident in their ability to get their work done, have positive, synergistic relationships with their tech, and experience less disruption in their personal lives.

This is a revolution that's happening for accountants in the industry. It's not just happening in the big conglomerates, but across organizations of all sizes. It's not every company yet, but it's a statistically significant percentage that we know is real. For some areas, it's not just 5% who are achieving these better outcomes, but 15% or even 20%. One of our hopes in writing this book is to help push these positive changes to a broader swath of the profession.

WHAT IS OPERATIONAL ACCOUNTING, ANYWAYS?

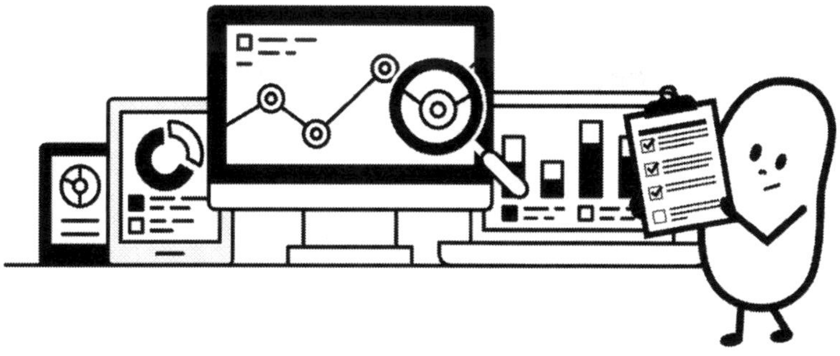

Stefan defines *operationalizing as measuring the abstract and tracking it with the intention of improvement.* What we mean by the abstract is all the separate tasks in a workflow that can be tracked and improved, from the minute things people just do, almost unconsciously as part of how they get their work done, to the 30,000-foot view of the entire process. This isn't just putting those tasks in a checklist to let people know what they need to do. The data we track isn't every minute nuance, but we track data with the intention to iterate and improve.

For example, if you're trying to improve the order-to-cash cycle, you might look at the process of how orders come in, and how they get entered in the system. How many touches by a human does this require? If you start at 10 touches per order, are there tools and process improvements you can implement to bring that to one touch per 10 orders or even one touch per 100 orders? By operationalizing that process — selecting a metric for improvement and tracking how changes to the process impact that metric — you can introduce small improvements that have ripple effects across the entire organization.

Operational accounting, as we'll explain in Chapter 3, means applying the skills we have as accountants for improving processes while also maintaining data integrity across the entire organization.

OUR START AT OPERATIONALIZING

Here at FloQast, our first head of operations was a CPA. Adam Schall followed much the same path as Mike: get a degree in accounting, work at a Big Four firm in audit for a couple years, then move over to a SaaS company, and see the need to do things differently. For Adam, it was Deloitte, while Mike was at EY. Unlike a lot of Big Four alumni, both Mike and Adam had really positive experiences, perhaps because they both want to keep learning and growing as accountants. Interestingly, Adam essentially took over the position Mike held at Cornerstone OnDemand as a revenue accountant before he left to found FloQast.

Adam developed an expertise in operations with his first big project at Cornerstone. He was tasked with implementing the Advanced Revenue Module in NetSuite. Before implementing ARM, they had "an army of accountants and billing clerks who reviewed sales contracts every month." First, a salesperson would create a Word document with the contract information for the customer to sign. Next, the billings team keyed the information into NetSuite, then the revenue team would review the contract and key it into a separate record in NetSuite.

Besides being highly redundant, the process was chaotic. The revenue team was continually following up with the sales team, the product team and the professional services team. "What did we really sell? What is the start date of this product? Do we actually have this product? Or is this on the roadmap?" Adam recalled. "It was very operational, very cross-functional. It wasn't just number crunching, but I was able to see all these different business processes, which, at the time I came on board, were mainly broken business processes."

By implementing ARM, the revenue process was largely automated. After the sales team keyed in the original contract data, no one else had to duplicate the work. The revenue team reviewed the calculations that ARM generated automatically and didn't have to do the manual work anymore outside of a few exceptions.

Adam discovered his true calling outside of pure accounting by focusing on process optimization, working with systems, and implementing technology. As he said, "Accountants should be the ones who identify and help fix those broken processes. The more we can streamline the repetitive work and automate it for accountants, the more we can free up accountants to do more of the strategic, operational work."

Adam came on board as our first (now former) head of operations about the same time we noticed that many of our customers were using FloQast to monitor operations outside of the close. According to Adam, we're a bit ahead of many other pre-IPO companies:

> *Most CEOs, and I'm generalizing, when they're trying to go public, they're really just focusing on revenue and growth and developing the product, which aren't the wrong things to focus on, but they still actually want to pay attention to operations. The fact that Mike had the foresight to invest in operations at this stage in the company's life cycle was what convinced me to come on board. I told Mike in order for me to really come on board, I had a list of things that I really needed, and one of them was a commitment that they were willing to invest in this department. Do not skimp on the team. I needed the commitment that they were willing to invest and actually hire because I had seen the flip side of working at a company where*

> *they didn't appreciate operations, and they would really be skimpy with headcount, which leads to less efficient and effective execution and crappy results.*

Internally, we've been emulating our clients who are using FloQast across our operations, rolling it out first to the office of the CFO.

CATAPULT YOUR COMPANY TO SUCCESS

We at FloQast believe that the controllers, CFOs, CAOs, and other key leaders in accounting who embrace the operational approach will be the ones who catapult their organizations to incredible success. Here's what Shivang Patel, another former auditor who now works as Vice President of Product Marketing at FloQast has to say:

> *I don't think that we realize the magnitude that an operational accountant can have on the business. Controllers are always running so fast. But if you have a good leader, and they hire a good team of operational accountants, things can get executed so quickly.*

By making accounting the center of operations, you have the ability to create a single source of truth. With an operational approach, your numbers are more accurate with each bottleneck you solve. Data is more centralized. Work is getting done faster. And you can probably save headcount as well. Then you find the next biggest bottleneck and solve that one too, chipping away at them one at a time.

HOW THIS BOOK IS STRUCTURED

Part 1, which is the meat of the book, explains what operational accounting is, and why accountants possess the correct DNA to take charge of this.

Part 2 describes what you need to do to move into an operational approach and how to create your playbook for optimizing operations.

Part 3 is our vision for the future. Our fervent hope is that by 2050, every COO will have come up through the ranks from accounting.

PART 1

WHAT IS OPERATIONAL ACCOUNTING?

1 / ACCOUNTING AS IT STANDS TODAY

LET'S ADDRESS THE BEANS

The public has almost no clue what it is we actually do. We're stereotyped as bean counters, as boring, nerdy introverts. What the public does know — or think they know — is that it's probably the most boring work that needs to be done. And, if they do think about what accountants do, it's almost always tax work. How many of you have been cornered at a party by someone asking for tax advice after you told them you were a CPA or accountant?

The public also thinks we must be math geniuses since we work with numbers. And if you're on the board of a not-for-profit, how many of you are the Treasurer? If we're lucky, the public will think of us as ethical, honest, and trustworthy. And if an accountant does find their name in a headline, it's most likely because of something bad they did, like Bernie Madoff and his Ponzi investment scheme or Arthur Andersen's work with Enron that torpedoed both companies in the early 2000s. Rarely are they celebrated when they perform heroics in saving a company from disaster.

Anyone who's worked as an accountant knows that this limiting stereotype of accountants as bean counters is way off base.

At FloQast, we fight a constant battle with outsiders and investors, even after 10 years of hiring accountants in every department of a tech company. Some of our outside investors can't understand that at FloQast, we have accountants in marketing, in sales, in product, in engineering — literally in every part of the company. We have a dynamic crew of accountants who are applying their skill set and knowledge base from their professional experience to areas far beyond producing financial statements.

Because FloQast was founded by accountants, we know accountants are a lot more than that stereotype of the introvert in the corner with the green eyeshade, working on that Excel masterpiece that no one will ever look at.

So let's change the branding of accountants away from bean counters. Starting today, let's change our branding to problem solvers. Process optimizers. Software implementers. Business consultants. Productivity enhancers.

The first step is to identify what we're actually good at and then capitalize on it. Keep in mind that what we learn in school is different from what we do in real life, whether we're in public or industry.

WE'RE GOOD AT SOLVING PUZZLES

Some of us majored in accounting because that's what one or both of our parents do. Others, who find their way to accounting naturally, enjoy working with puzzles. We grow to love the beauty of debits and credits balancing and the trial balance that emerges from the transactions. It's problem solving. It's applying theory to actual business transactions.

But the public perception is different. As we mentioned above, most people think that we must be good with math to be accountants. And yes, we know numbers, but the math is automated. You do not have to be good at math to be a great accountant. Excel and ERPs automated the math part of accounting 40 years ago. The most advanced math you might need is maybe some algebra.

Accountants are really good at solving puzzles. Double-entry bookkeeping and accounting are beautiful and complicated puzzles to be solved with rules, regulations, common sense, and discovering the patterns in the data. We can get really good at looking at financials and finding the problems, and figuring out how to plug the holes. Sometimes it's more thought-provoking than the hands-on work of creating pivot tables and writing formulas.

There's that exciting moment when you book that correct journal entry and everything balances and ties out. It's a little dopamine hit when that puzzle comes together. If you've never experienced that sensation, maybe you shouldn't have gone into accounting at all. But we all recall that first dopamine hit from the balance sheet when everything tied out and balanced. There's no way to describe that feeling to a non-accountant.

WE'RE CHRONICALLY UNDERSTAFFED, SO WE HAVE TO BE MASTERS OF EFFICIENCY

As we'll delve into in the next chapter, there's been a talent crunch in accounting for longer than either of us have been in accounting. The unemployment rate for accountants tends to be around 1%-2%, which is just people between jobs, or taking a breather out of sheer exhaustion. As the adage goes, "If you want something done quickly, give it to the busiest person."

We're smart and hard-working. Our deadlines are non-negotiable and we get it done. Even in the startup world — where Jaysen Dyal, FloQast Product Marketing Manager says "it's so fast-paced that you always feel behind the ball" — we find ways to complete what needs to be done.

The success we have in keeping the iterative process of the month-end close running and meeting the deadline every time raises our profile in the larger organization as leaders who can operate in an extremely pressurized environment.

Besides the disruption of the pandemic, we've made it through the new revenue recognition and lease standards. It's becoming second nature to look at our processes to see how they support the new kinds of information we need to report, without crushing our teams with more manual work.

WE KNOW THE REGULATORY ENVIRONMENT VERY WELL

We're experts at interpreting, implementing, and ensuring compliance with accounting rules and government regulations. We work within the compliance and reporting frameworks of the IRS, SEC, FASB, GASB, and IFRS, all of which constantly change.

Stefan says there are two ways the regulatory environment impacts us. First, there's a tactical knowledge of regulations. Second, the regulations form the foundation of how we move through the world. Let's look deeper at how Stefan understands these two ways.

First the tactical piece. The regulations and accounting standards help us take events from the past and record them in a universal language. They're like the Rosetta Stone. Raw accounting transactions are data, and the standards transform that data into information that people can consume. No matter how these business transactions occurred, we can translate them so other people can understand the impacts of those transactions. That's what we're trained to do. The regulatory environment is like the lexicon or the structure of our language.

When we first learn English, we learn what an apostrophe is, and that helps us distinguish between a possessive and a plural. That's literally what we do with the standards.

Accounting is our language, the language of business. That's the environment we grow up in.

Second, accounting forms the foundation of how we move through the world. The discipline of the regulations and the standards build up a strength in us that shows up in how we communicate and how we do things.

It's like farmer strength. If you've ever met a farmer, they have this deep strength in their body that's unrivaled by people who go to the gym every day. They might not be lifting 100 pounds at a time, but heavy repetitions are part of their daily lives. Growing up in Idaho, Stefan wrestled a bit in high school, and whenever he went up against a farm boy, he says "they were just denser than anybody else you met. It led them to be great wrestlers because they just moved weight all day."

Accountants have a kind of farmer strength when it comes to processes and interpretation of business regulations and accounting standards, because that's how we're trained. We just do it over and over again. So that strength makes us really great at other tasks, even though they're not directly related.

So if you look at operations, because we can understand the language of business, we can follow the flow of data and understand what's happening at each point. And because we deal with complex regulations, we know how to change and improve processes to make them cleaner — like a more concise sentence. For us, it's all about structure.

And especially in the world of startups, it's crucial to understand the standards and the regulatory environment. Jaysen Dyal put it this way: "No one's ever won a deal because they had clean accounting records. But deals have fallen through because of bad accounting records. A number that changes materially, that could kill a deal. No one's ever said 'Apple is worth more than Amazon because their accounting team is better.'"

WE LOVE PROCESSES AND CHECKLISTS

Most of us grew up in the audit world, where we lived and breathed checklists to make sure we didn't miss something material. Here in industry, we rely on checklists to get through the close and our other monthly work. Through our training in audit and our work in industry, we have come to possess the understanding and the ability to create and implement processes, procedures, and controls.

Over the lifetime of a company, the accounting team grows and changes. People come and go, and most of us eventually learn that the key to successful scaling is consistency, which requires well-defined and well-documented processes. This way, you always know that you're comparing apples to apples when you look at trends across reporting periods. Documenting processes is essential for ensuring continuity when team members leave, move to different roles, or simply aren't available to do their part of the work.

WE ARE DETAIL-ORIENTED

Anyone who has worked with contracts, leases, or any kind of business agreements knows that tiny details can make a big difference in how a transaction gets recorded, especially with the most recent revenue recognition and lease standards. Many of us came up through audit, where accuracy — or at least being materially correct — was drilled into us from day one. Lilith Chrakian, Finance Operations Manager at FloQast, says that emphasis on details and accuracy also can translate into a high level of client service. In her current role, she's responsible for onboarding clients in FloQast, and making sure that the trial balance and all the checklists are set up correctly. "There's that piece of client service that you learn in audit that translates across roles, where what you provide to a client has to be very accurate and professional."

One of the biggest things Lilith learned from her time in audit was "the review process, and being able to review thoroughly and efficiently, and to give really good feedback to help the people who reported to you." Focusing on the details in her feedback has helped her build a super detail-oriented team with the same commitment to client service, not to mention the confidence and ability to work independently.

Even though we are detail-oriented, controllers instinctively fear they may be missing something. As Stefan says: "Is there something happening in the company that affects us financially that I am not seeing? That can be anything from fraud to 'Has someone on my team messed up a report? Is the system giving me the right information? Is something broken and I'm not identifying it in time? Are my risk mitigations working?'" Many times, these problems are minimal, but that obsessive attention to detail helps us make sure that everything across the organization is working correctly.

WE'RE MASTERS AT HITTING DEADLINES

Our deadlines are non-negotiable. Missing a deadline can mean missing bank covenants and getting a loan called. When more work comes up, we just work more; that's how we respond. We have that farmer strength, so we just keep going. That's the attitude you want from anyone managing a deadline, so that puts accountants in a really good position. We can hold the company as a whole accountable for getting their work done, because we're already good at holding finance and sales responsible for getting their work done on a quarterly basis.

WE ARE MORE THAN BEAN COUNTERS. BUT THAT'S NOT OUR REALITY

This litany of things we're good at should destroy the stereotype of us as just bean counters.

Unfortunately, the reality of being an accountant doesn't always let us leverage these skills, whether we're in public accounting or in industry. In Chapter 2, we'll look at some of the challenges facing businesses that add to the pressure cooker we live in.

2 / THE PRESSURE COOKER OF ACCOUNTING TODAY

THE SKILLS we laid out in the last chapter should position us perfectly to be catalysts of change within our organizations. We know how to work when our teams are under-resourced. We're naturals at solving problems. We're detail-oriented, and we understand how to work within a complex regulatory framework. We touch every part of the organization, so we're in the perfect position to dissolve the bottlenecks. By transforming the raw data of business transactions into the information-rich financials we output every month, we provide the leadership with the foundation they need for decisions.

Yet the pressures of business today threaten that foundation. Let's take a look at those pressures, and at a few signs that our role is shifting, giving us the perfect opening to adopt an operational mindset.

BUSINESSES DON'T UNDERSTAND US

Businesses don't understand that our skills can be — and should be — leveraged to help improve their results. We're up against years of viewing accounting as just back-office work that has very little to do with the way the company makes money. Rather than being perceived as the profit driver we can be, the accounting department is often seen as nothing more than a cost center.

When it comes to company-wide tech spend, accounting usually gets the last bite of the apple. This often means that instead of spending a modest amount on software to automate a process, companies just expect us to grind through, so we get stuck doing a lot of manual work.

Companies keep us doing that boring work because that work needs to be done, but it becomes a vicious cycle. We're the recorders of history, limited to the rearview mirror perspective. We want to do the fun stuff (which is actually what companies need to stay competitive), but we can't find time to do the strategic work because we're buried in the close and in the reporting required for compliance.

Now, we're not downplaying the importance of those financials. As CEO, Mike relies on them to map out strategy for the company and to keep investors updated. Just like when you're driving at top speed on the freeway and you need that rearview mirror perspective to safely change lanes, leadership needs those financials to fully understand where the organization is right now.

What we're saying is that the skills we have also can be

applied to a front windshield perspective for the company. We can help everyone we interact with to see how the work they do is aiding in the company's forward momentum.

It's hard to find balance between the traditional reporting work that must get done, and stepping into a nontraditional role of trying to effect change within our organizations. It's hard to change the perceptions across the broader organization that would allow us to step into a bigger role.

The result is that most of us are trapped in that rearview mirror perspective. For those of us who are CPAs, it's more than a little aggravating that we spent all this time taking classes and studying for a super hard exam, and then we discover the reality of accounting in the real world. We and all the other very intelligent people in the accounting department get stuck ticking and tying, line by line. We're bogged down in details of transactions and endless reconciliations. With the incredible volume of transactions that come through most companies today, that work really sucks. We spend hours shuffling through email, looking for that damn approval.

That's not what we went to school for, not what we took the tests for, and not what we excel at. Instead of doing the analysis and higher-value work, we get stuck doing work that you clearly don't need a CPA or CGMA or even an accounting degree to do. No one — or almost no one — majored in accounting and got their CPA so they could spend their days crunching numbers and working on massive spreadsheets and wading through endless reconciliations.

We're not doing the fun stuff.

When we surveyed accountants about what they would do differently than today, they said they'd like to do more of the forward-thinking, strategic things that have impacts across their organizations, as the graphic below, reprinted from *Controller's Guidebook: When Accountants Dare to Dream*[1] shows:

Set the direction for projects or your work	83%
Make choices that impact the performance of your organization	78%
Have a valuable voice in strategic directions	76%
Bring your mind, thinking and perspective to your work	75%
Suggest future long term options that are not yet on the table	74%
Be proactive	74%
Take a wider view rather than staying down in the weeds	74%
Think about things in ways that transcend your finance role	71%
Make suggestions for achieving strategic objectives	71%
Be a catalyst for change within your organization	67%

How would accountants approach their job differently if given the opportunity?

All of these responses are the fun stuff, the things that businesses should be leveraging our skills for. But there's currently a huge disconnect between what we'd like to do and how leadership sees us: 67% of the accountants in our survey said they'd like to be catalysts for change in their organizations, but right now, only 26% feel that leadership from their organizations see them in that light.

Many of the people who want to do the strategic work get frustrated and leave. Sometimes they move to another company, but sometimes they leave the profession altogether, which means we have even fewer people to do the work. And, thanks to the infinitely expanding number of regulations businesses have to comply with, there's always more and more work to do.

EVEN CFOS AND CEOS MISUNDERSTAND US

A common misperception is that accounting only looks backward, while finance only looks forward. And that's how CFOs and CEOs tend to treat the accounting department. We're relegated to the rearview mirror view of the business while FP&A gets the forward-facing windshield view. But even in that perception, who's looking at the present?

The reality is that accounting is looking at the present to try to impact the future.

When Stefan was an auditor, he thought the audit was the most important thing. He thought those audited financial statements were crucially informative to the board. But when he got his first job as controller, he realized that the audit wasn't that important. He already knew that his financials were materially correct, that he had controls in place to prevent fraud and to make sure mistakes weren't getting through. By the time the audited financials were ready, the board and the C-suite had already seen the numbers for the last several months and had been making decisions based on the unaudited financials.

As controller, Stefan wasn't worried about getting the audit completed. He was worried about "what we can do today that impacts next month, that impacts six months from now, and that impacts a year from now." He was more concerned that the organization was making plans based on projections with a foundation in the single source of truth, and not just on a financial model spun out of partial truths by someone in finance.

Many CEOs and CFOs think that the numbers and facts and dashboard graphics they use for decisions are coming from finance when those numbers are actually coming from accounting. Finance was just the department that delivered it. The monthly financials and projections are more like a collaborative group project between accounting and finance, but, as Stefan has often experienced, finance tends to take full credit for the work.

But the forward-thinking controllers and accountants we're working with at FloQast are working to change that. They're pushing FP&A to give them a voice, and they're seeking out companies with collaborative finance and leadership teams. And the CEOs and CFOs are beginning to notice this new breed of forward-thinking accountants who, in reality, have always been there. It's just that we're finally being noticed.

EVER-INCREASING REGULATIONS LEAD TO EVER-INCREASING COMPLEXITY

FASB's recent overhauls to lease standards and revenue recognition has made us all-too-aware of the constant changes to accounting standards. The U.S. Congress and the IRS — like all other tax regimes around the world — keep adding new tax laws and regulations in an eternal quest to balance revenue generation with business incentives and economic fairness.

But those aren't the only areas of regulatory complexity businesses have to deal with. Depending on the organization, you may be subject to rules and regulations from the SEC, EPA, OSHA, FTC, FDA, FCC, CFPB, and the DOL, to name a few. And that's just on the federal side. Your organization may also be subject to regulations imposed by one or more states or countries. While those government agencies aren't all strictly related to accounting and financial reporting, because we interact with almost every part of the organization, those rules and regs nevertheless enter our purview.

Here are a few stats to put this complexity in perspective:

- Between 1956 and 2016, the U.S. population increased by 98% but federal regulations increased by 850%.[2]
- The estimated cost of compliance with federal regulations in 2022 is $1.97 trillion.[3]
- This is about the same as the sum of 2021 estimated individual income tax revenues ($1.7

trillion) and business income tax revenues ($268 billion), and nearly equals an estimate of 2020 pre-tax corporate profits for U.S. and international businesses ($2.2 trillion).

- As of Oct. 11, 2023, the Federal Register of government agency rules, proposed rules, executive orders, and other documents contained 87,803 pages.
- This is down from an all-time high of 95,854 pages in 2016.
- The California Code of Regulations for 2021 totaled more than 15,000 pages across 28 volumes.
- The U.S. federal tax code is 6,871 pages, plus 75,000 pages of regulations.
- In 2020, 34% of compliance teams worldwide spent 1-3 hours per week updating policies and procedures to comply with the latest regulations, and 26% spent 4-7 hours per week.[4]
- Between 2002 and 2014, the average U.S. firm spent between 1.3% and 3.3% of their wage bill on regulatory compliance.[5]

Keeping up with this complexity requires businesses to devote resources to compliance — resources that could otherwise be directed to moving the organization forward. And a good chunk of compliance with this ever-increasing Mount Everest of rules and regulations inevitably lands on our desks.

HIGHER SCRUTINY PUTS FINANCIALS UNDER A MICROSCOPE

Higher scrutiny comes in two flavors: internal and external. Internal scrutiny is a good thing. As a company grows, internal decision-makers become more knowledgeable about how the numbers work and how they relate to what's going on in the business, so they understand the financials at a deeper level every year. They think of new KPIs, and new ways of thinking about how the financials relate to the performance of the business.

The financials themselves become more sophisticated over time. Every few years, the effort that goes into producing the financials increases noticeably. We've seen this across the board in our customer base. Sometimes this occurs because leadership and the accountants are learning more and becoming more intelligent about the financials, and sometimes this happens when new, more experienced people join the organization.

Higher external scrutiny is an inevitable result of the increasing regulatory complexity we mentioned above. No matter who's in power, regulators never want to regulate less. They always want more insights into how companies are operating, and to rein in as many of the bad actors as they can — those people who are pushing the boundaries of what's perhaps moral and what's perhaps good business judgment.

Much of this increased regulation comes from the market wanting to mitigate risk. After catastrophic market crashes such as the one in 2008 or more recently, in the COVID era, investors want more guardrails to reduce the risk of losing their investments again. Over the last decades, regulators have been consistently pushing more rules and standards down to the auditors and the issuers of financial statements. We see this with updates to FASB and IASB standards for leases and revenue recognition, with updates to the PCAOB standards, and with the way the SEC interacts with auditors and scrutinizes their work. And soon, the SEC and states like California will be adding ESG reporting on top of what companies already have to report on. Organizations doing business in the European Union will have to comply with the Corporate

Sustainability Reporting Directive (CSRD) starting in 2024. Despite ongoing calls to simplify the U.S. tax code, that's not likely to happen in our lifetimes.

All that external scrutiny trickles down from the SEC and PCAOB to the auditors and from there, to the creators of financials. Audit firms risk losing their livelihood if they don't comply with all the rules and standards pushed down on them, so they in turn push the extra work down to their clients.

Both flavors of higher scrutiny require accountants to continually do more in less time, adding yet more pressure to our workloads.

VOLATILE MARKETS ADD TO UNCERTAINTY

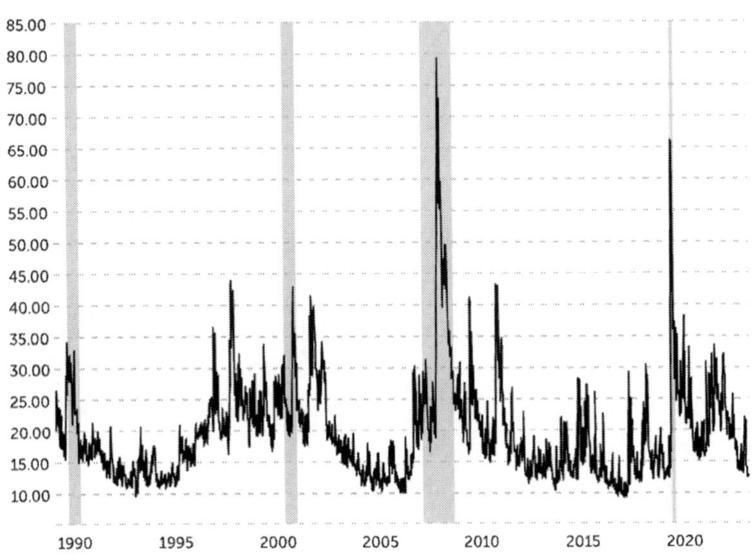

Chicago Board of Options Exchange Volatility Index

Since the early 1990s, the Chicago Board of Options Exchange (CBOE) has been tracking market volatility with its Volatility Index (VIX), which also is referred to as the "fear index." In general, a rising VIX is associated with increased fear among investors and falling stock prices, while a declining VIX is associated with decreased fear and rising stock prices. While the VIX, as reprinted above as of December 2023,[6] has been on a rough decline since it hit a high in March of 2020 (at the height of the COVID-19 pandemic), the rollercoaster bumps of the last few years have many of us wondering what will happen next, especially in the wake of worldwide political turmoil and ongoing fears of an impending recession.

This volatility adds to our challenges. The number one challenge for companies is cash flow, but uncertainties about interest rates and markets can make planning for the next five years — or even the next five months — seriously difficult.

Public companies may see their stock prices go wildly up and down, impacting not just their valuation, but their ability to raise capital. Investors may become risk-averse and less willing to provide desperately needed funds, and may demand steep interest rate increases or other concessions. Supply chains can be disrupted by currency fluctuations or availability of raw materials. Consumers may limit spending in uncertain times, or may simply have less money to spend. Borrowing gets harder when interest rates climb, or if market fluctuations impact perceived creditworthiness.

All of this compounds with the result that making strategic decisions for the organization becomes evermore challenging and anxiety-driven for the C-suite. That anxiety translates into pressure for us to close the books faster and faster to get the financials into the executive team's hands as soon as possible.

Dealing with the challenges of compliance and market volatility wouldn't be so difficult if we had enough time and enough people to do the work, but that's not likely to ever be the case, as we'll describe below.

OUR ALREADY TIGHT DEADLINES KEEP GETTING TIGHTER

The roller coaster changes of the last few years have ratcheted up the pressure to close the books faster every month. The businesses that survive and thrive in this crazy, post-pandemic world are the ones that can execute on changes faster, so the pressure is on us to get the numbers out sooner. Long gone are the days of the "leisurely" 20-day close.

Today, even 10 days can feel late. Unfortunately, there is no number that will satisfy business leaders. If you reduce your close from 10 to eight, and then from eight to five and so on, users of the financials will always want that information sooner. And, as we'll mention soon, little progress has been made in reducing the days to close in the four years since the COVID pandemic disrupted the entire world.

It's understandable that the C-suite needs the information quickly. Imagine driving on the freeway, but your rearview mirror has a five-second delay. That's what it's like for executives when they need to make decisions now, but won't have the information they need to make those decisions until the books are closed.

And if it seems like your auditors are getting extra demanding in their turnaround times for PBC items, you're not imagining it. Many, if not most, audit firms are trapped in a rapidly commodifying business model, so they need to make up in volume what they are losing in fees per audit. A few firms still give 30-day lead times, but most managers and seniors are just too busy to pick their heads up and plan out that far in advance, so the controller may only have two weeks to complete schedules and provide the other PBC items. However, to give ourselves a shameless plug, some of that time pressure can be alleviated by implementing FloQast Close and giving your auditors access to your instance, where they can find a huge chunk of the documentation they want.

THERE WON'T EVER BE ENOUGH PEOPLE TO DO THE WORK

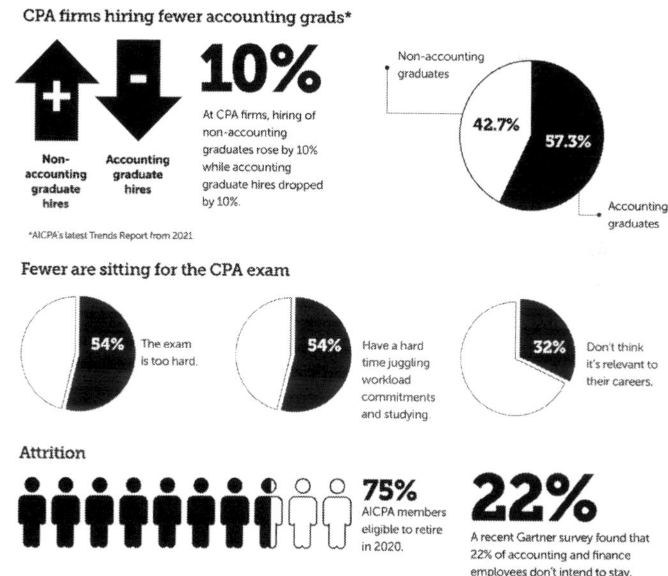

Since at least 1998, the Journal of Accountancy has been running articles about the "current staffing crisis."[7] Back in 2019, James Madison University's School of Accounting noted a 34% drop in enrollment in Intermediate Accounting, which is typically the weeder course for accounting majors.[8] And in the AICPA's Trends Report from 2021,[9] CPA firms dropped their hires of accounting graduates by 10% while hiring 10% more non-accounting grads. The hiring mix is shifting. Only 57.3% of new graduate hires are accounting graduates, while 42.7% are non-accounting graduates. Fewer students are graduating with bachelor's or masters' degrees in accounting, a trend that continues in the AICPA's 2023 Trends Report.[10] The number of people sitting for and passing the CPA exam is still trending downward, with only 18,847 candidates passing all four sections in 2022, compared to a high of 27,889 in 2016.

To delve into the reasons for the decline in people sitting for the CPA exam, the Illinois Society of CPAs surveyed more than 3,000 accounting students, graduates and professionals under 35. According to their respondents, 54% say the exam is too hard, 54% have a hard time juggling workload commitments and studying, and 32% of those who don't sit for the exam don't think it's relevant to their careers.[11]

So, fewer students are going into accounting, fewer of those are bothering to sit for the CPA exam, and at the same time, the baby boomer generation of CPAs is gearing up for retirement, if they haven't already done so. Meanwhile, 2021 saw a record 5.4 million applications for new businesses.[12] While that trend has leveled off somewhat, the U.S. Census Bureau recorded around 400,000 new businesses starting up every month throughout 2023.[13] Before the pandemic, it was fewer than 300,000 per month. All of which means that there's more need than ever for our services.

The talent crunch has been exacerbated not only by the all-too-accurate stereotype of accountants as bean counters, but also by an outdated staffing model. CPA firms and accounting departments in industry hire off the attrition model. The typical first-year audit staffer or entry-level accountant in industry gets loaded down with tedious, highly manual work. They're stuck doing tasks that do not require a degree in accounting, much less a CPA with 150 hours. Not surprisingly, there's a lot of turnover. Only a few people hired on as staff accountants at Big Four firms actually stick around long enough to make manager or partner. It's the same in industry, where a recent Gartner survey found that 22% of accounting and finance employees don't intend to stay.[14] Many of those who leave Big Four or accounting staff jobs do so out of sheer boredom, burnout from the long hours and a lack of clear career options in their current position.

Growing tech companies — like FloQast, for example — not only struggle to find enough great candidates to fill slots in the accounting department, but the few they do find face an ever-increasing workload, as our Controller Greg Vecellio explains. "Yes, you've got automation, but the day-to-day stuff keeps increasing." Since Greg came on board in 2018, we've grown from 140 people to more than 600 at the end of 2023. And like many tech companies with investor and board oversight, "It's the age-old thing," Greg says. "Nobody wants to spend money on G&A. When you go into the board, you want to say, 'here's what we're spending on sales, this is what we're spending on marketing. And look how little we spent on G&A.'" Adding extra headcount to accounting can be a tough sell.

Back in 2015, the AICPA estimated that 75% of its members would be eligible to retire by 2020,[15] which makes the average age of members disturbingly old. With fewer young people entering the field, the talent crunch is only going to get worse. It will be really bad in 10 years when people need to get a tax return done and they won't be able to find a tax accountant. Or when a company needs an audit and can't find an auditor at any price. Already, tax accountants and auditors are turning down business because they're too busy.

THE PANDEMIC MADE IT WORSE

Accounting teams have not been immune to the Great Resignation which the COVID-19 pandemic inspired. A 2021 survey by Spendesk of more than 1,000 finance professionals in the U.K., France, and Germany found that 40% of finance professionals might leave their jobs, with nearly half of those planning on leaving in the next year.[16] A survey of CFOs by PwC found that 81% were either very concerned or somewhat concerned about turnover,[17] with 83% citing hiring and retaining talent as the top key to growth in 2022. Even the Wall Street Journal has published articles about the 300,000 accountants who left their jobs between 2019 and 2021[18], shedding light on how job security is no longer enough to keep accountants in their positions.[19] And according to the accountants we surveyed in October 2022 for Chapter 3 of our Controller's Guidebook, 53% were not sure they'd be working for their current company for another year or two.[20] Even more troubling, of that 53% who were considering departing their current employer, 65% weren't sure they'd even stay in accounting another two to three years.

This should not have come as a surprise to anyone that highly educated, highly ambitious people would get tired of doing manual work and might reassess their opportunities, and that they might be experiencing burnout. When we surveyed accountants in March of 2022, 99% were experiencing some level of burnout, with 24% reporting high levels of burnout.[21]

Accountants today (and especially younger accountants) want work that has meaning. There's almost no value or meaning in the ticking and tying that consumes so much of their days. Plus, the younger generation is used to automating big chunks of their lives with their phones. As Jaysen Dyal, FloQast Product Marketing Manager, said, "People that are in public accounting are in a highly ambitious industry. You might start with 100 people, but only about two to three of those individuals that start in public accounting will go on to become partners, and from those two to three, maybe less than one will become successful at being a partner. I think during the pandemic, a lot of people were like, 'I'm gonna take my ambition somewhere else.'"

Some of those people took their ambition to FloQast. We've always had a high proportion of accountants working here, but our percentage of accountants went up materially during the Great Resignation. Overall, the Great Resignation continues to be good to us. We fared really well with good people not leaving, and we hired a bunch of unhappy people out of accounting and from the Big Four.

In fact, we hired nine people out of Deloitte in 2022, which was enough that they had to disclose it in their audit opinion and explain that it was not an independence violation. None of those new Deloitte people work in accounting. They're all in sales or recruiting or products. Over the years, we've hired a bunch of people out of the Big Four, particularly from PwC.

At the same time, the COVID pandemic brought out the need for companies to remain agile and able to function, even when key people leave. According to a 2021 survey by PwC of U.S. C-suite executives,[22] 48% were changing processes to reduce dependence on institutional knowledge. Nearly a third

(30%) were undergoing a major operational model overhaul. Among CFOs, 68% were increasing their investment in digital transformation, including cloud and analytics, continuing what they had been doing for the previous 18 months. More than half (56%) said these investments in tech would make their companies better.

But just investing in tech doesn't work miracles. According to a survey we did with Ventana Research in 2023, while firms invested in more tech when they were forced to go remote during the pandemic, "the adoption of new technology appears to have had no impact on accelerating the close compared to our findings in 2019."[23] About the same number of survey respondents in both years said they were able to complete their monthly close within six days: 58% in 2023 vs. 60% in 2019. However, for the quarterly close, which, as we all know, is more demanding, fewer were able to complete their quarterly close within six days: 44% in 2023 vs. 49% in 2019. The researchers at Ventana hypothesized several reasons for the lack of substantial improvement in four years. First, accounting departments lost headcount in the Great Resignation, so they are trying to do the same work with fewer people. Second, just adding tech without also optimizing processes and workflows does not lead to automatic digital transformation, especially when change management and training are given short shrift. This is even more true in the virtual environment, where many if not all accounting systems and processes will need to be overhauled.

This mirrors what we are seeing among the controllers we work with.The increasing complexity of today's business environment is pushing the days to close up, with no sign of trending down. At the same time, we are seeing pressure from management to close faster. So even maintaining the same days to close is a fragile status.

With fewer people around to do the work and a widespread

pivot to remote work, three in four controllers reported taking on more roles and responsibilities in 2020, according to a survey by the Controllers Council.[24] The biggest new role was supervising a remote workforce.

Remote work is here to stay, despite the demands from many companies to return to the office. Managing remote workers requires a different skill set than watercooler touch points and doing an end-of-day walk around the office to see who's still around and what they're working on. The lack of visibility into employees' work is fundamentally different than in-office and creates much bigger blindspots. It requires intentional touches to make sure everyone is doing well, and that the right work is getting done at the right times.

TECH TO THE RESCUE (SORT OF)

The good news: Software is automating some of the grunt work. The bad news: The technology that was supposed to make our jobs easier hasn't done so.

Technology in business tends to focus on automating the recording of transactions. It's only solving part of the issue. We've figured out how to get typical transactions into the GL with minimal manual effort. But as anyone in corporate accounting knows, that's not the end of accounting. There are a lot of non-typical transactions. There also are other things we need to do with the raw data to ensure it's consistent, complete, and reliable. Jaysen Dyal, Product Marketing Manager at FloQast puts it this way: "I think the industry analysts and the experts, and everyone thought that because accounts have an ERP system, accounting is done. But the truth is, that's just the beginning." You still have to close AP, close AR, calculate your accruals, and all the other upstream stuff that doesn't just flow perfectly and accurately into the financials.

What technology hasn't done a great job with is a holistic and systematic view of the workflows and the manipulation required to move the data from transaction to reporting. And the need for this view of accounting is why forward-thinking controllers were hacking FloQast Close to manage their workflows — and that is what inspired us to create FloQast Ops. It's why we're pushing toward the next frontier of tech in accounting: the operational approach, which enables accountants to monitor, manage, and improve workflows across their organizations to make things better for the people in those organizations and the organizations as a whole.

Without a whole-business, operational approach, all these siloed parts of a company are using tech that might make someone's job easier, but they don't always play nicely together. The data outflows from one app don't always include what we need to do our jobs easily or efficiently. It's like throwing data over a fence and not caring what happens on the other side.

When Mike was at Cornerstone OnDemand, the functions under the CFO were pretty siloed off. "Finance did their thing, the controller did her thing, and all of us assigned to different areas would do our things," says Mike. "The only way we would collaborate was when something was messed up, and someone would come ask me a question about it. There was no ops mentality of trying to make it better next month." Workflow management and the ops approach will be the missing key that will ultimately support and enable accountants to do the strategic work — the fun stuff that stretches them beyond the current state.

The average accounting team probably has anywhere from 15 to 30 different applications they use on a day-to-day basis.. These apps range from a host of specialty modules such as payroll and AP for the ERPs to spreadsheets, email and collaboration. According to Colleen Wanty, our former Senior

Director of Product Marketing, "in survey after survey, accountants still report their jobs continue to involve a lot of manual work, even though this is 2024, not 2000." Colleen has observed the ERP market over the years, and while they have evolved, she still asks "How is it, with all these applications, accountants are still reporting, in survey after survey, that they still continue to spend a lot of their time on manual work." This was only exacerbated with the pandemic and the advent of remote work.

With the rise of Software as a Service (SaaS), tech buying decisions have been democratized across the business buyer and IT organization, with business buyers becoming much more involved in the process. Colleen notes that "finance and accounting teams who used to be *part* of the technology buying process are now *driving* technology purchases."

With SaaS, the old model of IT-driven evaluation and installation for software purchases has completely changed because the burden of evaluating technology compatibility and installing software is significantly decreased.

"But," Colleen continues, "finance and accounting teams traditionally lack experience in evaluating, purchasing, and implementing software. They often have high purchase regret because they may not know how to run an evaluation or how to go through the change management process, which is often a huge pitfall with new technology implementations, whether SaaS or not. This is even more apparent with the rise of a new role in larger organizations – the Finance Transformation Manager – whose focus is helping with this exact need."

A great example of this is when the controller or CFO buys and implements an ERP, and they think it will solve all their problems, but then reality hits. Colleen explains: "ERPs are a core application in the finance technology stack to capture and classify transactions at volume. But ERPs don't do so well in specialized functions like sales tax, where you might need a sales tax application to ensure compliance with the thousands of sales tax jurisdictions across the U.S. and globally. And across record-to-report, you might need other specialized applications to handle accounts receivable, revenue, and equity."

So, to summarize: Businesses misuse us by forcing us to do boring and repetitive work, because they don't understand the skills and knowledge we possess. Ever-expanding regulations add to the complexity of business. Tightening deadlines force us to work under intense pressure. Volatile markets require constant agility, and we're hampered by tech that doesn't always play nice together. All of this creates a pressure cooker environment that makes us more robust as accountants, but also runs the risk of breaking us.

CFOS AND CONTROLLERS ARE MOVING INTO OPERATIONS

The good news is that for years, CFOs and controllers have been moving out of roles as strictly bean counters. As a sign of the increasingly operational and strategic role of today's CFO, in 2020, only 36% of CFOs of the 1,000 largest public companies were actually CPAs, the lowest proportion in the six years since Korn Ferry has been collecting that data,[25] as reported in the Wall Street Journal by Mark Maurer. Even at FloQast, when we finally hired a CFO, we hired one who came up through finance, not accounting.

Maurer reported that this move accelerated after the 2008 financial crisis, "when companies increasingly wanted strategy-focused CFOs who would promote transparency and operational changes to spur growth and guard against threats."

This new generation of non-CPA CFOs are taking on more of the work that used to be the work of the CEO. Some of this is happening because CEOs are becoming more of a brand ambassador. With a more public-facing role, they are less able to oversee the strategy. So as the work gets pushed down from CEO to CFO, CFOs are taking on more responsibility around operations and IT. On our podcast, "Blood, Sweat, and Balance Sheets," we recently hosted Actian Corporate Controller Dante Giannini, who talked about how the role of CFO has been changing dramatically over the last 20 years:

> *It's grown from being 'Where do we invest? How do we invest in the company and grow our product and grow our base? And how do I fund those things further?' to having those operational elements. I think the CFO role has become more of an Operations Officer role as well. And they're starting to think about, well, if I'm investing in this, how are we achieving operational excellence and how does this stuff move and flow? As that role has grown and changed, that's then what ends up driving some of the change in the controllership role. Because naturally, they're going to want to hand off some of that responsibility. They'll need somebody to support and drive their additional responsibilities.*

They can't give all this work to the VP of Finance or the head of SEC reporting, so it needs to go to either the controller or to the FP&A team. Of those two choices, the controller is the better fit, as Dante continued:

> *I think more of it's falling to the controllership because the FP&A side really is more about 'How do I advise the business?' not 'How are their processes working?' whereas the controllership side needs to understand how the processes are working, because all of that data flows into my financials. And I need to make sure that those processes are clean and efficient, so that my team, who's at the end of it, isn't getting crushed, and that our financials are accurate.*

Dante said this transformation has been happening much more in mid-size companies. Extremely large companies with headcount of 1,000 or more usually have a COO who has their own team that focuses on operations, but even in those large organizations, Dante believes "the controller needs to partner tightly with the COOs, because all of that stuff is still going to be driven into the financial systems. And so that relationship needs to be extremely tight. And those two people need to be walking in tandem."

Some companies are intentionally broadening the scope of the CFO position as a retention strategy, as described in a recent Wall Street Journal article.[26] The average CFO stays on the job about five years, so in the midst of a tremendous talent crunch, companies are broadening the roles of CFOs as a means to recognize, engage, and retain their second or third in command. As of June 29, 2022, 30 of the S&P 500 CFOs had additional roles: "Of those 30 finance chiefs, nine had additional operational duties, two were their company's vice president with expertise in specific areas of the business, or chief strategy officer, and 19 were also division chief executive or president." This is an increase from 2020, when only seven of these 500 CFOs had additional operational responsibilities.

As CFOs take on more responsibilities, something has to give. They want to do more of the strategic work, not the tactical or the operational. So to get work off their plate, the person they delegate it to is the controller.

We know this is happening because when Mike talks to investors, they all understand that the CFO is getting more operational responsibilities. So he positions it as "we're all aware that the CFO is now being asked to do not only finance, but strategy and now operations. A lot of companies don't even have COOs these days. And what we've seen is CFOs like that work the least. As such, they delegate it to whoever makes the most sense. That is the controller. And so we're seeing that play out with our client base."

THE RISE OF THE OPERATIONAL ACCOUNTANT

Controllers around the world have been taking on more challenging roles, moving out of the strictly transaction-related work and doing work that impacts the direction the company is headed. And we're seeing the most innovative and forward-thinking controllers moving to the ops mentality.

The ops mentality isn't about outputting more work. It's about gaining an in-depth understanding of how your organization operates, and finding ways to make those operations work better for everyone. It's not just about getting those financial statements and metrics out more efficiently — though that is a definite advantage — but about smoothing out the bottlenecks and kinks so the whole organization runs better. It's also about gleaning insights from subtle shifts in the business, the industry, and the overall economy to better inform higher-level organizational strategy. Some of that is using tech tools, some of that is deploying people to the bottlenecks, and some of that is developing processes and systems to streamline how the work is done.

Whether we want it or not, operations are increasingly coming into our sphere of influence. "Controllers today are finding that they're overseeing a bit of finance and reporting and a bit of tax in the workflows, and they're responsible for tracking people and processes," according to Adam Schall. They're using collaboration software to track what's going on across their companies. They're collaborating across what used to be silos to find ways to make processes smoother and get the information faster. They're identifying and solving the hidden issues, then making future processes better. They think about the problems they have, maybe with downstream users like finance, and relate it back to another problem. By solving that problem, they can make the future process better.

The job of the accountant will still be to produce the financial statements and metrics that executives need to make decisions. The operational accountant will still do that. In addition, the operational accounting will be more involved in the increasingly sophisticated and detailed internal reporting that companies need as they grow. Because the accountant is operationalizing the workflows that produce those financials and metrics, the data will be reaching leadership sooner. And, since more of that reporting is passing through accounting, it will be more reliable because it will be based on a single source of truth.

As we mentioned above, the relentless pressures of deadlines, regulatory complexity, talent issues, and market volatility, create a pressure cooker environment for accounting. This pressure, however, isn't all bad. Like the pressure that turns coal into diamonds, our ability to deal with these competing stresses while executing with excellence has long been one of our superpowers. It's our farmer strength, as Stefan calls it.

Accountants have been navigating these pressures for the last 20 or 30 years. We've ridden markets to their highs and to their lows, and we've met these challenges. Anyone who rises through the ranks to become controller or CFO will tell you that dealing with these unrelenting pressures has been instrumental in creating the powerful leader and robust accountant they have become.

Today's pressures, however, are more powerful. With too much pressure, eventually the stone will crack.

But by leveraging technology, collaborating across silos, managing workflows, and smoothing out bottlenecks, operational accountants are using this pressure to become diamonds. We are still in the early innings of this game, but this change will only accelerate. The work of the controller will never be less operational than it is today.

In the next chapter, we'll take a deep dive into exactly what operational accounting is and how moving into the operational approach will help you move out of the strict bean counter role and help you become a catalyst for change in your organization. Instead of breaking with the pressure, you'll use that pressure to become a diamond.

3 / WHAT IS OPERATIONAL ACCOUNTING?

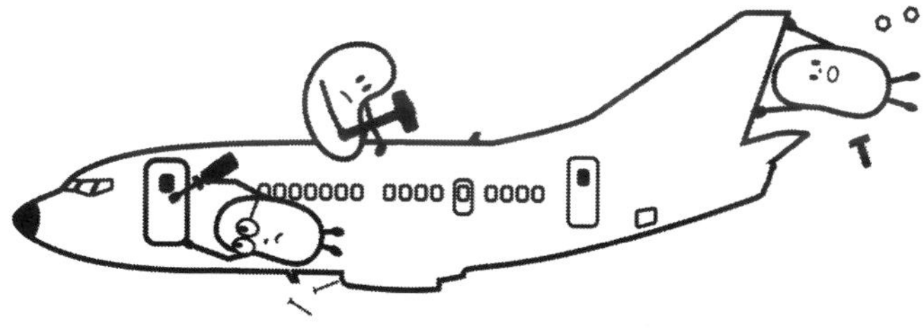

You're flying the plane and trying to change the parts at the same time.
—Mike Whitmire

WHAT DOES operational accounting actually mean? Operations is the playbook for how to run your business. At a startup, operations can be a "catch all, not something that's very well defined," according to FloQast co-founder and Chief Product Officer Chris Sluty, who took on that role as the three co-founders — Mike, Chris, and Chief Technology Officer Cullen Zandstra — were getting the company off the ground. "If nobody's doing it, then operations can kind of take the ball and run with it. So at least early in my career, there was a lot of 'Hey, somebody needs to do this.' So, OK, I'll figure it out."

As companies grow, operations become more like "internal consulting for a business," according to Adam Schall. "You need a breadth of knowledge about the company to understand the ins and outs of the business so you can connect the dots in business processes and systems and data from one department to another," he says. "Each of the functional departments has depth of knowledge about their particular function, but the operational accountant knows how those functions connect. They act as the guts to connect all the business processes and data and systems." Accountants are a natural for this role, because we already have to connect all these dots in our monthly accounting.

That old trope from Mike at the top of this chapter may be a really lame one, but it perfectly captures the idea. Your destination is the source of truth, so you keep an eye on the incoming data and do what's needed to keep the plane flying.

The way we define operations in this capacity is the things that happen on a recurring basis that have a deadline. We're not talking about the one-off approval processes or things like that. What are the recurring activities of the business that keep everything running? What makes up the regular cadence of the company? We can take the skills we described in Chapter 1 and extend those to the rest of the organization to keep people on track and make the business run smoother.

DEFINING OPERATIONAL ACCOUNTING

Operational accounting, narrowly defined, is taking the process of operationalizing, and applying it to the operations of the office of the CFO to improve the speed, accuracy, and usefulness of reporting to company leaders. But in this book, we're taking a broader stance and extending the purview of the operational accountant to the organization at large. As we'll discuss in Chapter 5, we believe that accountants are the ideal ones to take on the role of monitoring, improving, and establishing the operational norms across the entire organization.

As Stefan defined it in the introduction, to operationalize is to measure and track the abstract with the intention of improvement. It means taking a fresh look at a process, and letting go of the notion that just because we've always done it this way, this is the best way to do it. Even if a process does not appear to be broken, maybe there are ways to make it better, faster, easier, and less manual.

What follows is an overview of operationalizing, which we cover in more detail in Chapter 8, when we present the FloQast Ops Playbook, but we're presenting it here as a bit of orientation to the whole process.

The first step in operationalizing is to **know what you are doing.** What is the purpose of the process you're trying to improve? Where does it fit into the overall flow? Is it dependent on particular inputs? Where does the output go? Are other processes dependent on that output?

Next, **determine what you need to track.** We're not tracking every minute nuance, but only the things that can be improved. Try to only pick one at a time. Often, fixing one problem area has cascading effects through other parts of the process, and may even have impacts in other areas. To identify the best attribute to start with, ask yourself a series of questions. Are there particular pain points or bottlenecks in this process? Where are the highly manual areas? What typically goes wrong? Where are errors introduced?

The attribute you choose to track might be more of a global bottleneck for the process, and not just related to one part of the process. For example, in our earlier example of the order-to-cash cycle, the chosen attribute was "human touches per order." How many times, on average, did a human need to do something to get a customer order into the system for processing? Other global-type attributes might be "number of processing errors" or (one of our favorites at FloQast) "days to close."

A common gripe from public accounting escapees is the relentless focus on the inherently meaningless metric of billable hours worked. Mike left EY when he put in 2,500 billable hours in one year, which made him #1 in the LA office. We've both heard stories of CPAs choosing the least efficient way to complete a project because they need to reach a weekly billable hour quota or, likely more frequently, eating hours because they've already blown way past the time budget. Billable hours is a meaningless metric because it doesn't necessarily add to the bottom line. Most audits are priced upfront by proposal, so the hours it takes to get the audit done has little to do with the revenue it generates. For other services, the partners freely write up or write down a bill according to what they feel a client will be willing to pay. It's also not a metric that helps a firm improve over time, largely because the numbers are not trustworthy. Never mind that accounting firms rarely analyze this data with the intention of improving efficiency.

While a significant component of operationalizing your business does require measuring and tracking things, the genius of an ops approach is that you're tracking something with the intention of changing it. You're using checklists to measure your workload and track it to see if there's a better way to do it, whether from the point of view of efficiency or quality or allocation. It's putting in place an expectation of what the team — the employer and employees — is responsible for, with the intention of improvement. It's not being used as punishment, but to make things better.

Now that you've chosen your attribute for improvement, **create a method and metric to track.** Ideally, this is something your system already tracks, or is something that your system can be configured to track. But sometimes this is something that has to be manually tracked, like our example of the number of touches per order. In this case, you'll need to get buy-in from the people who will be doing the tracking. They may need reassurance that their position in the company won't be eliminated when the process is made more efficient.

Next, you need to **determine goals** for improvement. You may first need to establish a baseline to see where you are now. Do you want to improve by 10% or 100% or 1,000%? Depending on your baseline and your chosen metric, any of those might be reasonable. You'll also want to add in a time frame. Over what period do you want to achieve this goal? Over a week or a month? Over a quarter or six months? Or by a certain date in time?

Finally, **create a plan to change.** How do you intend to achieve this goal? By implementing tech? By streamlining a process? Or by standardizing a process? Who will take ownership of this improvement plan? Who else needs to be involved? What information do they need? Will they need training? How will this training take place?

Once your goal is achieved, **rinse and repeat.** Operationalizing isn't a one-and-done thing. This is an iterative cycle that can be continued basically forever, or at least until something else rears its ugly head.

Operationalizing is an overt expression of change culture. It incentivizes your team to challenge the status quo and to find ways to make things better for everyone. You also can make this rewarding for everyone, whether just from making work a better experience or adding a cash bonus or recognition for outstanding work.

Instead of chasing after meaningless metrics like working an insane number of hours, you flip the old public accounting mentality on its head. You don't want anyone — not you and not anyone on your team — to be working long hours, but rather getting the work done as efficiently as possible so they can have a life outside of work. This can become a great strategy for retention, by the way.

Here at FloQast, if a team member suddenly finds they have extra time, that's OK. We can find something else for them to do, something that's more enjoyable, and maybe something that can become a mission. Our highest goal both in how we operate as a company and with our products is to take people away from mundane tactical tasks so they have the time freedom and mental bandwidth freedom for more interesting and strategic work. Both sides win: The employee gets more enjoyment out of their work, which means the employer gets more out of that employee.

Operationalizing means identifying and deploying the technologies for process adherence and mass processing of data — the things machines do best, and letting humans do what they're best at: the creative, the problem solving, and the new.

We're not looking to reduce the human element in the workforce, but we want that human element to grow and become better human beings. So let the machines do what they're good at, and let the humans do what they're good at.

That's how you build a company that succeeds. That's how you transform your people into strategic assets.

THE THREE PARTS OF OPERATIONS

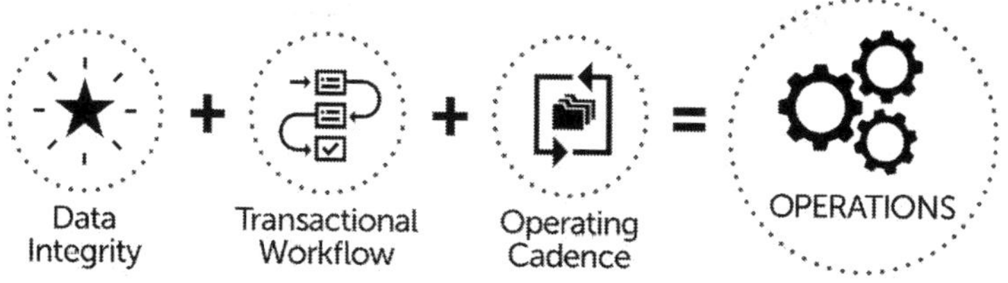

Fundamentally, ops is three things: data integrity, transactional workflow, and the overall operating cadence of the organization laid on top of everything. Let's look in detail at what those three things are.

Data Integrity

Data integrity means that there is a single source of truth that serves as the basis for all the reporting and metrics used by all the departments. One of the challenges we had at FloQast was every department had their own datasets they would use. Customer Success had their own means of getting data about what our customers were doing, what churn was, and the other data points that helped them do their jobs. Sales had their own data around pipeline, funnel, leads, and conversions. Finance had the numbers and metrics and really was a source of truth — or should have been what everything else connected to. It was fine for a little while that every department had their own set of data.

Then we hit a point where the numbers were not reconciling across board presentations. We had a couple of meetings where board members would call us out: "Hey, why does your main board deck say your net revenue retention was 112%, but your customer success deck says it was 111%?"

We were having issues around data integrity and our data not being centralized. So we brought Adam Schall in to nip that problem in the bud before it got too bad. He worked on getting the information out of departmental silos and making sure that all the systems are using the same information and aggregating that information into one central repository, which is owned by finance. That repository serves as the source for all the numbers and metrics and all the reporting and information requests that everyone from the executives to department managers use. Now the leadership team can be confident that the decisions we make are based on what's really happening at FloQast.

Both of us have seen issues from our audit days and from previous companies where people were not looking at where their data is coming from, so they were not using a single source of truth. And sometimes, like the example of the 111% versus 112% for NRR, it's close enough that materially it doesn't matter. But sometimes those differences can be big enough to make a significant difference. What if the assumption of inventory on hand for a manufacturer is materially incorrect? That can result in drastically over-buying or under-buying specific items. Data integrity can impact running the company as well as profitability.

And if you're planning to grow even bigger, or possibly merge with or be acquired by another company, the problem just gets worse, especially when you have subsidiaries in other countries, where you have not just intercompany issues but battles with foreign currency.

Transactional Workflow

Besides the usual workflow that happens every day, there's bespoke workflow. This is for things that don't necessarily happen every day, or even every month or quarter. These are things that come up and you need to take care of them, and you want some control behind it. A good line of delineation for when you need to create a standard process for something is "does this require an approval?" One easy example is someone wanting to make a new hire. At the beginning, we were totally casual, and Mike would just promote someone on the spot. But for SOX compliance purposes, we need a documented process.

There are a lot of very specific things we need to do to hire someone or even promote someone internally. First, we need to request the headcount from finance and HR to get a position opened up and a salary range approved. Then we write a job ad and post it. Then someone weeds through resumes to find the candidates to interview, and after interviewing everyone, we make an offer to the candidate who's the best fit and ultimately make the hire.

That's a whole workflow that should be standardized. And everything that goes into that should be very repeatable. Along the way, we have to document all the different steps we need to comply with.

Another workflow is expense reimbursements. When we were really small, it was a hyper manual process, where Mike would give the controller his credit card statement, maybe once every nine months after he'd been sitting on it forever. As we grew, we needed to put controls in place, not just from a compliance perspective, but also because it's not really scalable and from a general expense perspective, we needed more controls and less volatility. If we don't give the salespeople good guidance around what they can spend money on, our budget can easily go through the roof without us really being aware of it. Now we have a whole process that's formalized and uses Coupa instead of paper receipts and Excel, with different approval thresholds for different people, and rules around what's approved and what's not.

General purchasing is another area where we had to develop a bespoke workflow. It used to be that if someone wanted to buy a piece of software, they could just get Mike's verbal OK, and sign the contract. We didn't pay much attention to the length of the commitment or whether that was really the best product for us. In the early days, Mike just wanted it to happen quickly. But now that we're bigger, we hired someone to be in charge of procurement. So now if you want something, you have to submit a request that explains why you want something. It needs to go through multiple vendor reviews, and the agreement negotiated appropriately with sign off by legal.

Operating Cadence

After seeing that FloQast customers were hacking our product to monitor and manage workflows across the company, another lightbulb moment for Mike was when he heard David Sacks talk about The Cadence.[1] This was a scheduling and planning method David learned first as COO at PayPal, and which he later executed as CEO and founder at Yammer, to make it one of the fastest SaaS unicorn exits.

The Cadence is a blueprint for synchronizing all the parts of a company so that everything is working from the same overall playbook. By applying The Cadence, in just four years, Yammer scaled to 500 employees and $56 million in annual sales before being acquired by Microsoft in 2012 for $1.2 billion.

Using The Cadence, you sync up the quarterly financial

reporting with the other activities of sales, marketing, and product to keep all the parts moving together so that the company meets its goals. Finance has its quarterly schedule of the reporting that needs to happen, and we work closely with sales to set targets. Sales is the team that the investors and the board care most about.

Unlike a lot of startups that don't think that way, this is exactly how FloQast started, at least in finance and sales. We had goals we tracked every quarter that we tracked against, we did quarterly business reviews (QBRs), we closed every month and every quarter, and we presented our quarterly financials to the board. It felt like very normal stuff to Mike as an accountant. But apparently, a lot of startups don't operate like that, and consequently, a lot of them get shaken out.

While we've been good about the finance and sales calendar from the beginning, when we first learned about The Cadence, we realized we weren't always so good about the product and marketing calendar. This has been super interesting to Mike, because, as an accountant, "it's common sense to keep sales and finance on track. You have targets that happen every quarter. But then there's this notion that product and marketing are the functions that support you being able to hit that number." Just to make sure the business is running normally and progressing, you want to set quarterly goals and deadlines for each of those departments as well.

The Cadence is all deadlines, which we understand intuitively. However, applying deadlines to product and marketing so they sync with finance isn't something we always understand. But when you know that something has to happen by week six of the quarter, you can work backward to see what has to happen in sequence to make that deadline.

Establishing an organization-wide operating cadence is something that's not really necessary, but all of the best companies have a regular quarterly routine. We'll go into more detail about The Cadence in Part 2, where we talk in detail about creating your workflows.

WHAT IS OPS RESPONSIBLE FOR?

At a top level, Ops is responsible for creating and documenting processes. But Ops goes deeper than that. The biggest problem in organizations isn't just designing the process, but making sure that the process aligns with reality so that people will actually adhere to the process.

Process adherence is actually a big problem in companies, because there are always external factors and pressures that are trying to change the dynamic. And if you have a lot of churn in employees, that just adds to the adherence issue. Even in a stable industry, people are always moving to new roles and new opportunities, so you have to build in that expectation of having to teach new people the process and getting them to do it consistently. If we have to change the process, we need to work with the people actually doing the work to make sure that the end path stays the same. It's the responsibility of Ops to be a bulwark against the external pressures to keep the machine fine-tuned and running well.

Optimizing processes is never a one-and-done project. In today's world, we have a dynamic business environment and constantly shifting regulations, so businesses are always changing how they do business. Anytime there's a change in how a company operates, that disrupts the flow of data. Which makes it really important to have that person with accounting knowledge who understands the process from record to report in charge of Ops. The new change may mean that instead of going directly from A to B to C, maybe now the best order is A to C to B. For operational excellence, it's crucial to have someone in operations who sees the big picture and who excels at adapting to every situation.

Making that dream vision a reality requires that anything that touches the financials be under the controller's purview, according to Dante Giannini, Corporate Controller at Actian, who talked about the rise of the operational accountant on a recent episode of our "Blood, Sweat and Balance Sheets" podcast: "In my mind, [operations is] anything that hooks into the financial system." Dante continues:

> *I think that's why you're starting to see more of these operational things starting to fit under the controller, because the controller now sits back and says, 'Hey, this information from SalesForce is flowing into NetSuite, and I need it to flow in a certain way. But I don't have the influence that I would need in order to make those changes.'*

For a tech company, this means the controller needs to work closely with sales leaders to get them the information they need, and to "be flexible enough for them to drive business without handcuffing them for what they could say are arbitrary rules," as Dante puts it. He continues, "but then make sure that we're capturing the data correctly" and that the data then flows through to the financials correctly, in a way that is meaningful, quick, and accurate "but doesn't crush everyone."

The places where operations touch accounting is where accounting needs to have a voice. For a tech company, that would be commissions and sales, while for a CPG company that would be inventory procurement. Although accounting is a critical piece of the work, it's not all that Ops does.

Our former lead of Ops, Adam Schall, breaks the operations team into three main segments. First, there are the general systems, the folks who maintain Salesforce and your ERP and access to the main systems you use to run your business. Then there's business intelligence, which is things like running reports for pricing strategies or other analytics for the executives to consider. Then there's general operations, which is sort of a catch-all category, which includes project managing certain initiatives, or coordinating information exchanges between several departments that are all working together on some larger corporate initiative. As your team grows, and your responsibility for Ops expands, you'll need dedicated team members for each of these segments. We'll talk more about these three segments of an Ops team in Chapter 9.

Another bigger part of operations is the responsibilities around the cadence of the business. Ops is what keeps the engine of the business moving forward. We'll go into the details of the cadence in Part 3.

THE HOLY GRAIL OF OPERATIONAL EXCELLENCE

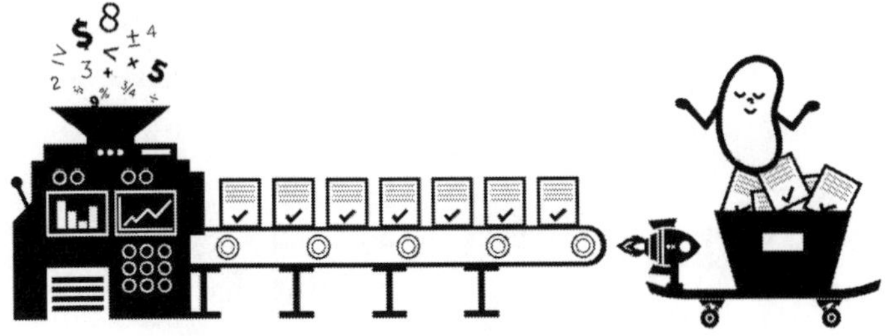

Operational excellence, as we reference in this book, is more a state of mind than an achievable goal. It's not that everything is perfect at your organization, but you've created an agile and consistent system for continuous improvement. You're collecting data and analyzing it. You're iterating and changing in a systematic way by following what the data says, not what your gut instinct might tell you. Following the data tells you when you're doing well and when you're not. You're following a process that helps you tune in the signal from the noise to understand what changes make things better, and iterating on those changes.

Operational excellence is a cultural mindset that's not content with blindly following SALY or the way we've been doing things for years. You're creating a culture that's open to change and that relies on data to tell you whether a change is good or not. Maybe SALY really is the best way, but until it's validated with data, anything and everything is ripe for adjustment. And with the rapidly changing business landscape, even if SALY is the best process today, it might not be the best tomorrow.

Maybe a change will succeed, but maybe it won't. You won't know until you try something new and let the data tell you whether your idea will pay off or not.

Businesses that are stagnant and stale, that aren't able to make the agile shifts needed now and in the future, will die. This is true for all organizations, all teams within every organization, and every individual on those teams. As executive coach Marshall Goldsmith says, "What got you here won't get you there." Everyone needs to be constantly iterating and adapting and changing, and as soon as you stop changing, you've given up.

The thing about operational excellence is that it's an ideal. There's no final level where you can be perfect. You're always chasing after an ideal, like what the Greeks called *arete*, which means striving to be the best you can be. You're looking to unleash the potential of the organization as it currently exists and to lay the framework for it to be even better as it changes and grows.

While there's no end state with operational excellence, there are two ways to think about it. The first way looks at the current state and how that can be improved by pondering questions such as: What do we have in the way of operational debt? Can we identify our biggest bottlenecks, and how do we clean those away operationally? With this perspective, something like the close analytics we have in our product can be really helpful.

You're working on continuous improvement. It's the approach of "water wears away stone," where continuous incremental improvement over time creates a smooth surface.

The other way to look at operational excellence is the forward-looking perspective. When there's an initiative coming out or a new direction for the business, you need to look ahead and structure things properly so that you don't ever accumulate operational debt in this new area.

With either perspective, there's never an endpoint. No company can achieve a perfect state where there's no room for improvement. Perfection is just not a thing, plus it's not a good mindset to have.

Operational debt happens a lot with startups, where the focus is on getting stuff done, not on creating processes that can scale because the investment in IT infrastructure isn't worth it when your priority is closing deals and getting stuff done.

We are certainly guilty of that. In our early days, the priority at FloQast was to get the work done right now and close some deals, rather than think about operations. An example is that we didn't take advantage of the integration between Salesforce and NetSuite, which meant a lot of duplicate work.

Our sales team uses Salesforce to track opportunities. After a deal is closed and the contract is signed, that information lives in Salesforce. The new contracts get handed over to the accounting team, who enters the sales orders into NetSuite, and does the invoicing.

That's how most people do the work. That's pretty much

the way it was done at Cornerstone OnDemand when Mike was there, as Adam described in the introduction. It's not ideal, because you can connect Salesforce and NetSuite to automatically create sales orders and automate invoicing, making it a much less manual process. But as a business, early on, we decided it wasn't worth the investment in IT infrastructure to have it operate like that, right out of the gate.

Fast-forward six years, and we've accumulated a bunch of operational debt. We're at the point in our company lifecycle when it makes sense to clean up operations because it's only going to get worse from here. We're at a point in the business where we can commit resources to help with that operational debt. Using our close analytics tool, we could see that our biggest inefficiency in accounting was duplicating the sales order and invoicing process, so we've prioritized that as the number one piece of operational debt to clean up. So we have a project underway to automate that whole process. It's a big project, and one that will take longer than some others, but when we have it wrapped up, that will be two fewer employees, just by automating that process.

At the same time, we also need that forward-looking perspective because we're launching into new territories and geographies. So we're looking at the things we can do today to get those new territories operating out of the gate as efficiently as we do in our offices across the U.S. We want our new offices to be taking advantage of the processes, procedures and technology that we already have in place in headquarters in LA, so the investment in IT infrastructure makes a ton of sense today.

OPERATIONS IS A MINDSET SHIFT

Accounting is the historical recording of what happened in a business. We're always looking at the past. We're looking at the rearview mirror to see what happened last month, last quarter, and last year. And that's an essential function for accounting. Typically, the accountants are at the end of a process, and they see everything as it's gone through all the processes.

The operational approach is shifting left in your thinking. It means being involved upfront and having the perspective of the downstream impacts. You need to think about how the upstream decisions made in different parts of the company will impact the recording and reporting of those transactions. It's a shift from just looking at what comes out at the end to being involved in the actual work being done, as it's being done, and in the decisions that are made, as they are being made. One outcome of that on the accounting side will be cleaner books because you've thought about the impact of operational decisions upfront. It's getting everyone in the business on the same page from the beginning.

The most interesting outcome is that because the accounting is cleaner, controllers and CFOs can position themselves to take a more active role in operational decisions because they now have the bandwidth. Shifting left means moving out of the tactical and into the strategic.

You can apply the dual perspectives of operational excellence we discussed above, not just in looking at operational debt, but at the transaction level. Jaysen Dyal says it's looking at the same event from two standpoints: "At the same time that you're asking, 'How do I report this?' You're also asking, 'What are the implications from an operational standpoint?'" From the operational standpoint, you have to understand what happened and how it happened. From the accounting standpoint, you need to know how to report it.

Shifting left means talking to those in your organization to find out what's happening in its different sectors. It's not just reconciling a GL account, but also understanding the business trends as well as existing and potential problems. Shivang Patel says, "Operational accountants have to keep the lights on, and also understand when and where to install new lights." Taking a more operational role is partly about making your own role bigger so that you're not just buried in the debits and credits and closing the books every month, Shivang continues. Instead, "you're looking at 'How can we make this piece work better?'"

The operational mindset also means being willing to look at things from a new perspective, as Jonathan Hardy, Director of FP&A at LeadVenture, discovered early in his career. "I was brought onto a team where most of the people had been in their roles for five to 10 years. And my boss told me, 'You're the newest person we have. We need fresh thinking.'" As Jonathan was being trained, his boss instructed him to always ask, "Why do we do it this way?" If the answer ever came back as "because that's how we've always done it," Jonathan was to make note of that process as something that was "ripe for updating and trying to figure out how to do it better."

For Jonathan, that early demand from his boss is how he views his entire job: "How do I do this better and more efficiently? And how do I challenge my team to do the same?" That mindset has helped him build a team of accountants who think holistically about processes "not just in terms of how do I go through these steps, but why am I doing it? What is the output and the ultimate answer people are looking for? Where's the data coming from? What steps could be different to make it more efficient?" The Ops approach forces his team members to "really understand what you're doing, not just how you're doing it" as a means for driving real improvements in the business.

When you move from public accounting into industry — as so many controllers have — you shift from being a revenue center to a cost center. But with the rise of operational accountants, you're not solely a cost center; you become a value-add driver. You're helping the company do everything it does more efficiently so that it can keep doing what it does.

When you're in public accounting, you put a lot of importance on the audit opinion and compliance with regulations. You are conscious of the possibility that if you don't give this organization the audit opinion they want, they might go under. The bank might call their loan because they didn't meet one of the loan covenants.

But when you're in an operational accounting role, your perspective changes. You don't really care so much about covenants and audit opinions because that's the past, and the past has been set. You can't really change it.

What you do care about is making sure the company is there tomorrow. You want to make sure you can make payroll, that the company is growing and that you have enough funds to buy inventory or to make that big investment. It's a mindset shift for the accountant and a shift in the value they bring to the company. You realize that this stuff in the past is relatively easy to manage and maintain once you get the process set up. The beauty of having those processes set up in a way that you can monitor what's going on is that you don't have to look at it too much. You can spend your time looking ahead to tomorrow.

Another trait controllers may bring with them from audit is the tendency to see things as black and white, right or wrong, with very little room for anything else. But as Hugh O'Neill, Sales Engineering Manager at FloQast, learned from an early mentor, "In the real world, there's elements of gray. You have to be comfortable operating in the gray." While many accountants may be most comfortable when each day is routine, the unpredictable nature of a business means that "quite often, you don't know what you are facing into," Hugh continues. "So it's going to be quite exciting for some people, but it can be quite terrifying for others."

Being flexible and willing to adapt to changing conditions is key to being effective in operations. It's also key for collaborating with other departments. To work well cross-functionally, you need to operate in some gray areas and be reasonable about the controls that get put in place as you scale as an organization.

One specific example where operating in the gray is especially beneficial is contracts. Accountants ask the sales people, "Why can't every contract that we sell be the same? Why can't we just get customers to sign the contract and move on?" But when you talk to sales, they'll tell you that every customer is different and they're just trying to close a deal. It's the real world. Different people want different things and so the sales people try to get the customer what they want.

So, accounting gets frustrated with having to translate every contract into GL entries and invoicing, and sales gets frustrated with accounting for wanting everything standardized, and you end up with a lot of headbutting. But maybe there's some reasonable middle ground so that sales can do their job effectively and make the accounting side easier.

That's where operations comes in. Instead of demanding that sales follow these black and white accounting rules, you can take a collaborative approach. You can set up rules of engagement, and parameters that everyone can work with. We still have to build a business, and closing new customers is an important part of that business. If your rules or parameters are limiting them and not enabling them, then you're probably not doing it right, even if you think you are.

So rather than having accounting dictate how sales does their job, work on finding a middle ground by developing operations around sales that act like guardrails. You're not dictating how sales does their job while also not holding them back. Keep in mind that we all want the same thing: to book revenue.

Much of the complication with contracts comes from how sales bundles things and how they discount. So the compromise we've gotten to with our sales organization at FloQast is to set up certain discounting rights that depend on your level of employment. So if you're a sales rep, you're allowed to discount up to the first level. With manager approval, you can discount a little more, and as you get approvals higher up the chain, you can discount more.

This has been a really good way of getting accounting and finance what they want, which is not just constantly discounting to close a deal, but giving sales enough flexibility to be able to do that on a call rather than getting every single discount approved by accounting or finance.

So that's a good example of FloQast being able to operate in a gray area, whereas some other finance departments are way more black and white than that.

Another big part of the mindset shift is not pointing out the places where people are doing things wrong, but finding solutions to make it easier for them to do their jobs more accurately.

Ops is not a finger-pointing exercise. It's taking the reality of where we're at today, and coming up with ideas to make it better.

Moving into Ops means you are constantly taking a step back and thinking about how any decision is going to impact the business, not just your job and not just you personally. And that that can be a difficult distinction for anyone to make, but it's especially important in operations.

Now accountants haven't always been eager to change. Coming up from public accounting, the first acronym most of us learned was SALY: Same As Last Year. But since 2002, when SOX took effect, accountants in industry, especially in public companies, have had to change how they work because the regulations became more stringent. Accountants had to change and improve, and that's become the new mode for accountants.

OPERATIONS IS THE BRIDGE BETWEEN STRATEGY AND IMPLEMENTATION.

Simon Sinek uses the model of a Golden Circle in his book *Start with Why* to explain the difference between companies that are amazingly successful and companies that fail. The Golden Circle is three concentric circles. The center is **Why**, meaning, "why does this company exist?" The next ring is **How**, which is "how does the company do this?" Finally, the outermost ring is **What,** which stands for "What does this company do?" In Sinek's model, when you have all three circles aligned, magic happens. Sinek's favorite example is Apple, whose **Why** is challenging the status quo and thinking differently. **How** Apple does that is by making well-designed, easy-to-use products, with attention to design details. **What** Apple does is make computers and other electronics.

Applying Sinek's Golden Circle here, **Why** is strategy, **How** is operations, and **What** is the implementation or execution. Ops is how you get stuff done.

Your **Why** is the thinking behind your current offerings.

How you do that is the work behind the scenes to move from concept to customer deliverables. **What** your organization does is execute on those deliverables.

For FloQast, our **Why** for writing this book is to help controllers elevate their accounting game through better, more meaningful work that provides greater satisfaction and improves their work-life balance. **How** this book accomplishes that is by providing a pathway to becoming an operational accountant. Our **What** is the book you hold in your hand.

As an example, let's talk about the contract to payment process from a slightly different angle. We keep revisiting this particular process because it's frequently a huge pain point for companies, especially as they grow. Mike saw this at Cornerstone OnDemand, and Stefan saw this at both Skull Candy and Kodiak Cakes.

Your **Why** is the vision behind the particular offerings you provide your customers. According to the language in ASC 606, you recognize revenue to the extent you have met your obligation under the contract. A company needs to give the customer what was promised under the contract. This is the **What**. **How** you meet the obligation is operations.

Accounting is measuring that performance and recognizing revenue in parallel with operations and ensuring that everything is done correctly.

Here's the dream vision. The process kicks off when a sales rep creates an opportunity in Salesforce or whatever CRM they're using. When the deal closes, they mark it as closed, and in a perfect world, that feeds into your ERP and creates a sales order. That sales order has the appropriate invoicing terms magically appear and has all the appropriate contracts attached, so revenue is recognized appropriately, the customer is billed, and the product is supplied.

The reality is a bit different. The sales rep closes the sales order, but they don't know what they're doing, so none of it makes any sense. Accounting takes the sales order and tries to reconcile it against the contract and figure out what's actually going on. Accounting has to manually enter those sales orders into NetSuite or Intacct and create the invoicing rules. Then accounting has to figure out revenue recognition manually because every SaaS vendor oversells on their ability to do allocated revenue for SaaS companies. It's all done manually with a bunch of walk-throughs and narratives about how this process is supposed to work. Those narratives become your playbook. Oh, and each contract also goes through a legal team to get the contract negotiated and a professional services team to onboard and support the new customer. As Adam Schall says,

> *Often the accountants see what broke along the way and what they need to follow up on. The operational accountant is the one who bridges the gap, connects the dots, and proposes process improvements, system improvements or just data recommendations.*
>
> *All of the data, process, and technology problems just fall on the accounting team. Because we're at the end, we can understand all the points along the way, which makes us the best ones to connect all of the dots.*
>
> *The operational approach is not just getting the sales contract at the end, but they work with the sales team so that they understand how a contract works in the accounting system, with the company's finances, and they work with the legal team and product so that everything is lined up.*
>
> *Bookkeeping is at the end, but a true operations function can advise and consult on what those business processes should look like, end to end. You're inserted along the way in a more centralized role.*

Connecting all the dots is a process. It won't happen overnight. You have to build out the processes to make things happen.

When he started at Cornerstone OnDemand, one of Adam's first projects was to get everyone on board with a quoting tool for the sales team. While the tool had been implemented, it was only used about 20% of the time. The rest of the time, the sales team was entering contracts in Word documents. He even had a tale of part of a contract package being a scanned PDF of a napkin with the contract information, signed by the sales rep and the customer.

To improve the adoption rate, Adam first worked to fix problems with the tool that made it hard to use. Then his team built out dashboards and reports that they could show to leadership. Through those measures, Adam and his team brought adoption from 20% to 80% within a year. With enough people using the tool, that made it possible to integrate the tool with the ERP so that the billing team no longer had to key in the data from contracts.

The operational approach is putting together the people, processes and systems so that the dream vision becomes the way that the company operates.

Here at FloQast, Adam's work came full circle. Before he came, our systems weren't integrated — except, of course, for FloQast, which has been part of our close process since day one. We didn't even have a quoting tool, so Adam led the charge to launch the Salesforce CPQ quoting tool. With that as a foundation, now we'll be able to move on to integrating the rest of our systems. As Shivang explains, launching CPQ took a lot of teamwork and cooperation across the company.

It involved five different departments, and business operations was the glue in the middle that connected all the dots and gave all the different departments their respective updates. And it was a long, arduous process.

As the bridge between strategy and implementation, Ops is "the center of what's going on within the company," according to Jerry Raphael, CFO of Hypori. Because he's connected to all parts of his organization, he can give his team in accounting a heads-up when something is coming, "whether it's a contract change or a process change that's going to impact the way they do things." Aligning all parts of the organization helps everything run smoother and faster.

OPS MEANS YOU GET TO DO THE FUN STUFF

The Ops mentality means you get to be a value add, instead of purely a cost center. Adding value is a huge boost to team morale. It's way more fun to spend time troubleshooting the reasons why tech and the people over in another department aren't getting the right information into the GL than to manually reconcile or record transactions.

Accounting is the process of recording historical events and analyzing what happened in the past to understand why things turned out the way they did. But analyzing the past can be limited.

For example, if you run your car into a ditch by accident, that's the past. That's often where accounting starts and ends. It's like sitting helplessly in the backseat of the car. After the car ends up in the ditch, all you can do is get the car out and try to move forward. The Ops approach is keeping the car from going into the ditch in the first place.

This is the more exciting part of Ops — the opportunity to be involved with setting that future. You can be part of the meat of the business and play a role in making this company the next big thing. Everyone feels they provide more value when they can see the impact of what they do rather than just sitting in the backseat and seeing what happens, hoping that the car doesn't end up in a ditch.

When he was on our "Blood, Sweat and Balance Sheets" podcast, Dante Gianini also talked about how being in the operational role was different from his previous roles. The interesting part for him was interacting with people in sales in a different way. Before, as Corporate Controller, his interactions with the CRO and sales were along the lines of "How do I help you structure your deal so you don't trip over any red tape?" But since switching to an operational role, he reported that he became more interested in understanding what motivated the sales team, how the deals came to be, and how the deals were structured. In the operational role, his thinking shifted to "How do we move things through the system in a consistent manner that people can rely on?" so that the accounting team could look back and understand why the deal was structured in a particular way. For Dante, the Ops approach means "thinking about 'How do I make these processes repeatable for things that can be unique?'"

Shivang Patel was an operational accountant at Ruckus Wireless at the time when the company was implementing SAP, and he served as the liaison between finance and accounting on one side and the SAP folks on the other side. Ultimately, because he had acquired a firm grasp of how SAP worked, he was the one responsible for training all of the global accounting and finance teams in how to use SAP, which was among his most valuable experiences: "I was able to travel to 13 subsidiaries and implement SAP in 13 different countries, which required understanding the accounting, tax and business regulations. That allowed me to understand really how the business operates. And I was at the helm of it."

At one particular meeting at the Bangalore subsidiary, he was in a conference room with 15 people: "I kid you not, they treat you like a rock star when you show up at an international subsidiary. My name was on a huge whiteboard with my photo, and it said 'Welcome to Shivang from HQ.'" At that same training meeting, he ran into a problem with SAP:

> *So here we are in a working session, and cash management was the topic. And I was teaching them bank reconciliations. There's about 15 people, and I ran into an error in SAP. And here I am, I don't have the ability to diagnose that error because the SAP Support Center is 12 hours different from us. And so immediately, I have a room of 15 people, not knowing how to do their job, and they were all leaning on me to understand. And I can't quite put it into words, but that feeling was one of excitement. But also, oh my God, I need to figure this out. The reason why I bring this up is because I think that feeling is indicative of an operational accountant.*

Being in operations isn't an easy task, according to Shivang. "It's always, a fire is lit under your butt. And how much are you going to burn?" Good operational accountants always manage to put those fires out. Shivang continues, "It's being able to operate under pressure, know what the strategy is, and yet still be able to execute at the drop of a dime. And that's not an easy task."

A common project for Ops is integration after a merger, which may mean involvement with completely different sectors of a business than we accountants usually have contact with. While Adam was at Cornerstone OnDemand, they acquired their biggest competitor, and he played a big part of the integration management office. Besides syncing up sales and finance processes, they had to integrate everything so that on day one, all the employees from the acquired company and Cornerstone would be able to log into the same systems and have access to the same tools, as if they were "all brand new employees who were part of the same company."

Another challenge was that the "acquisition resulted in a lot of synergies, which meant job cuts for folks. ... The unfortunate task of letting go of people and figuring out the timing of that was very, very different from a lot of the system and process work," Adam said. For that task, Adam worked closely with R&D, finance, and the executive team to set targets for how many people from each company to retain, while also working with the Chief Product Officer to ensure they hit the targets while also delivering on the product roadmap. The very last piece of the integration was to bring together the business systems, which don't get integrated on day one. To make matters more complicated, the acquired company had itself acquired a company the year before, but had not fully integrated that, so it was like bringing three companies together.

Other projects that you might be involved in as an operational accountant include being part of a team to develop new business lines, which can include pricing those new products and forming partnerships with others. Adam did this at Cornerstone OnDemand when they began working with third-party content providers who wanted to use the Cornerstone learning management platform to provide their training materials to a wider audience. One of Adam's responsibilities was figuring out how to pay their third-party partners. Under their prior model, the customer would purchase something like a sexual harassment training course, and Cornerstone would pay the partner a portion of the purchase price.

However, Cornerstone wanted to move to a subscription model more like Netflix, which was great for the customer but, because payments to their content partners were based on consumption, it was difficult to track operationally. He worked with the content team, the accounting team, and the sales team to figure out how to go to market with it, how to pay their partners, and how to operate the back end. There was no tool to use to track that, so it was a painful process.

On our podcast, Dante Giannini described a meeting with all of the C-suite at Actian about a new product called Avalanche Cloud Data Platform. In the meeting, they discussed non-accounting questions such as "What's our go to market strategy on that? How do we support the SAS product that we're putting out there? How do we make it meaningful for our customers? How do we price it? How do we do all of those things?" While corporate controllers sometimes get to see those things, Dante's role as an operational accountant allowed him to participate in discussions about pricing metrics, revenue recognition, information flows through the system, and the reporting metrics they would use to measure performance, as well as find ways to motivate the sales reps in ways that excite them, but don't destroy the profit margins.

As an operational accountant, you also can be the bridge between strategy and execution for the C-suite. While the C-suite is responsible for setting strategy, they don't always have a good lens on execution. Acting as that bridge is an immense responsibility, and it shows your value-add to the overall organization. It's an exciting role where you can see how you're impacting financial statement items. Besides your own role, you also will naturally elevate the roles of the whole team, which helps everyone get out of the mundane and into the cool stuff.

WORK HARDER OR WORK SMARTER

Mike says there are two types of controllers and accountants he's worked with. There's the group that just puts their head down and grinds through the grunt work, reconciling transaction by transaction, or putting together a bunch of pivot tables. It's highly manual, and extremely time-consuming. It's easy to get lost in the details. But they're comfortable working within the lines. That's their sweet spot. And don't get us wrong — the world needs them. They get stuff done. They get the books closed so the company can keep going. Shivang Patel calls these the technical accountants. If you're reading this book, you're not likely one of these.

The second type of accountants are those who pick up their heads and look at the problem with the end goal in mind. These are the ones who work smarter, not harder. Shivang calls these the operational accountants, and "they don't cross paths" with the technical accountants. By thinking more intelligently about the problem they're trying to solve, they find ways to solve the problem more efficiently. These are the controllers and accountants who are focused on getting the work done more efficiently because they see that the objective is not just following the steps in the process to get the work done, but to get the output of those processes into the hands of the people who need that information as quickly as possible while still retaining accuracy. The controllers with the Ops mentality are always trying to make their department and their organization better and more efficient.

Operational accountants are the glue that connects everything in a business. They know how the guts of the business connects everything in ways that the teams outside of accounting don't know. Because they work cross-functionally, they know every little nook and cranny of the business. They develop an understanding of operations across the organization.

Shivang acquired this understanding in his job as Accounting Manager at Ruckus Wireless. One of his first assignments was to perform a completeness test and make sure there was a reconciliation for every account. Before he could do a reconciliation of an account, Shivang first had to understand what the purpose of the account was. In order to gain that understanding, Shivang would sit down with people doing the work and ask them a series of questions, starting with the basics of what they did in their job and what their role was within the company. Those operational exercises helped him develop a deep understanding of the order-to-cash process, from entering new sales orders through invoicing, packing and shipping the order, and ultimately processing the payment.

CHANNEL YOUR INNER LIONEL MESSI

Undoubtedly, some of you reading this book will be objecting that you can't possibly take on a bigger role in operations when you're already running at top speed just to get through your regular work. There's just no time. You can't run any faster or push any harder than you already are.

What we are saying — and what we've observed with the forward-thinking, Ops-minded controllers and CFOs we talk to — is that the Ops approach lets you be more like Lionel Messi.

Lionel Messi is one of those great soccer players who even non-soccer-fans have heard of. He's Argentina's all-time leading scorer, with more than 800 career goals. In 2012, he scored a record 91 goals combined for Argentina and Barcelona. Time Magazine has named him among the 100 most influential people in the world three times — in 2011, 2012 and 2023.

Yet there's an oddity about the way he plays. Throughout his career, he's been criticized for walking much more than other players. Overall, he runs less than most comparable players. During a 90-minute game, he typically covers about five miles, while most others are in the six- to seven-mile range.

Messi seems to have a deep perception of where everyone is on the field relative to the ball and the goal. He understands the flow of the game better than most other players. He's not constantly running to the ball. Instead, he's creating space for his teammates to pass him the ball at the right moment.

He's figured out how to win more games by working less.

The Ops approach lets you be more like Lionel Messi. You will perform significantly better while working less.

With the Ops approach, you will be increasing your depth of perception about the organization and you'll become more involved in operations. Trust us, this will not make your life worse. The Ops approach will make your life better, and it does so in an exponential way that you may not believe is possible.

The Ops approach means you acquire a deep understanding of your position within the organization and the capabilities and capacities of your team. You'll look at certain issues and you'll know you don't have to be involved because your team can handle it. But what you do need to be involved in are the issues that seem trivial now, but which have the potential to cause big problems in the future. By having that broader field of view, you can use your judgment to tackle issues before they get out of control. You're making sure that you are in the right place at the right time to make the opportunity happen.

In this chapter, we've just touched on the many possible impacts you can have as an operational accountant, and the kinds of projects you'll be taking a lead on. Instead of just counting the beans, you'll play a role in creating the beans, and helping your organization multiply those beans. You'll be channeling the energy that gets wasted on broken and inefficient processes into moving forward. And you'll achieve more with less effort.

As we've worked with controllers and CFOs across the country and around the world, we've noticed a number of telltale signs that an organization isn't functioning as optimally as it could. In the next chapter, we'll discuss those symptoms, and over the rest of the book, we'll explain how the Ops approach can fix those problems.

4 / SYMPTOMS THAT YOUR ORGANIZATION NEEDS THE OPS APPROACH

While we believe that every company would benefit by focusing on Ops starting from day one, that's not the real world. Even here at FloQast, we didn't find that Ops focus until recently. New companies tend to be chaotic, as everybody just works to get stuff done, product out the door, and the books closed. Companies that have been around a few years or decades often have processes that have been used since forever. On the surface, things look OK, but probe a little deeper, and you may find some telltale signs that you need to switch to a new approach. Such signs include:

HAVING NO SINGLE SOURCE OF TRUTH

At FloQast, it broke for us about two years ago when some of our board materials did not agree cross-functionally. Our Customer Success team had one number, but our finance team had another number. It was embarrassing and not a good look for the board, especially from a company with accountants in every department. So we needed to get it sorted out.

CHAOTIC DECISION-MAKING

If you're not using correct data, that can show up as an inability to make sound decisions. This is especially true if you want to be a data-driven organization, which most people like to say they are. You need actual, good data to make data-driven decisions. Poor decision-making can be the result of having poor data.

THROWING MORE BODIES AT THE PROBLEM

This is a classic symptom of needing an operational approach. When the response to every new problem is to open up a headcount, you know something's not right. Mike saw this at Cornerstone OnDemand. Instead of spending $30,000 per year on a tool to help manage contracts, they just kept hiring Big Four auditors at $70,000 a pop to do the work. If they had used software, they might have only needed three or four people to manage revenue instead of the 11 Cornerstone had when he left. It made zero sense.

Throwing more bodies at the problem hasn't been a viable solution for some time. There just aren't enough bodies out there. Hiring accountants is becoming increasingly expensive, and unless the organization offers extraordinary benefits or an awesome culture with true work-life balance, those bodies you do manage to hire are likely to take their ambition elsewhere the minute they get a better offer.

TURNING TASKS INTO JOBS

As you scale, some people might get a little overworked because new things are continually put on their plate, yet nothing ever gets taken off. So you open up a headcount, and ask what they need help with. However, when you look at the job description for what they want to pass off, there's no way that someone would need 40 hours a week just to take that one task off someone's plate. This is a really dangerous thing around organizations, and it can lead to bloat.

We had that happen here at FloQast, and we did a big open headcount cleanup. We looked across G&A and found a lot of open positions where tasks had turned into jobs. For one of the positions we had open, that new person would have worked maybe two hours a week, with a crunch time at the end of the quarter. It was definitely not a full-time job. By consolidating tasks, we were able to combine several open positions into one headcount. Doing that required having cross-functional conversations about what an actual new hire would be doing, and locating the redundancies so that one headcount could be assigned the different tasks to create a full-time position.

Other ways to solve that would be finding software that takes over part or all of the task or outsourcing the task, maybe to your law firm, or finding a gig worker or freelancer to do the work. But you don't have to take on a full-time headcount to solve every extra task put on someone's plate.

EXPERIENCING AUDIT ISSUES

If you're failing controls, or if you're getting a significant deficiency or material weakness, that's a very good sign that you need to start cleaning up operations. This is a no-brainer. If you have a material weakness, you need to get an Ops person in immediately. Even if the auditors just threaten to give you a significant deficiency or material weakness, that should be enough of an indicator to take a serious look at Ops. Failing controls is always a symptom of poor operations.

With auditors, it can be a pretty confrontational relationship. But the reality is they have a lot of experience. Your auditors can actually provide excellent insight into how much help you need on the operations side. Companies really should leverage their audit firms more by having a good post-mortem with their audit partner. In our experience, a good way to get that insight is for the CFO or controller and the audit partner to have an open conversation about what went well and what went poorly during the audit. You might even drop down to the audit manager, because a lot of information gets filtered by the time it gets to the partner. But the audit managers are the ones in the weeds reviewing the work papers, and they can tell you what's really going on.

If you hear a lot of issues around the control side of the audit, your spidey sense should be going up. You need to be thinking about investing more in the operations side of the house. Even if you don't get a control weakness or a threat of a deficiency, you want to nip those problems in the bud. You want to avoid bigger problems happening down the track. Cleaning up those issues early can help you save big on audit fees. If you're a public company, you definitely don't want to get a control failure, because your stock price will take a hit, and your investors will definitely not be thrilled if they find out you're not running a clean shop.

This is also something you should think about when you're selecting an auditor. When you're talking to the audit partner, you need to get a feel for their approach. Is this a gotcha partner who is trying to find problems? Or is it more of a relationship partner? Will they be willing to give us ideas in comparison to other clients, or are they going to give us the lowest fee so they can get in and get out as quickly as possible? Despite the trend for audit to be highly commodified, there are audit firms out there that offer more than just an audit report. Look for these firms, preferably one that has expertise in your industry.

If any of the above symptoms sound familiar, keep reading. Through the rest of Part 1, we'll explain why accountants should be the ones leading the charge, and in Part 2, we'll cover the skills you'll need to thrive in Ops, and teach you how to shift toward this approach.

5 / WHY ACCOUNTING SHOULD TAKE OVER OPERATIONS

IF YOU LOOK at the job postings for VP of Operations, most often you'll see that a business degree or maybe a computer science degree is required. But rarely do you see accounting or having a CPA as a requirement. Maybe we're biased since Mike is a CPA (albeit inactive, as the state of California requires him to state) and Stefan also got his start in audit, but we think accountants should be the ones running operations.

However, what happens in a lot of companies when they want to fix their operations is that they hire one of the big consulting firms like McKinsey or Bain to come in and tell them what to do. But as we'll explain here, that's probably the worst way to make things better.

WHAT THE CONSULTING FIRMS GET WRONG

Mike has never been a fan of Bain or McKinsey or any of those organizations. His gripe with them is similar to his gripe with audit. As those of us who came up through audit experienced as first-years, we get thrown into the field without much more than textbook ideas of how accounting happens in the real world. So when we as super-green auditors go and tell the controller that they're doing their job all wrong, without any real understanding of how accounting gets done, the controller's response is to smile and pat you on the head and say, "That's cute. Glad you read that in a textbook or picked that up from a different client. But that doesn't work here. Our company is different for XYZ reasons. Give yourself a couple of years and you'll learn."

It's the same scene with the Bains and McKinseys of the world. All those big consulting firms hire a bunch of MBA kids out of Ivy League school who read a bunch of case studies about big companies as part of their coursework. These kids out of college have never actually worked within the operations of a company, so they're just applying textbook and portfolio bias to their engagements. As green auditors (hopefully) eventually learn, it's way different to work within a company, come up with ideas to improve things, and then actually execute on those ideas and make sure stuff happens.

Those kids come in and tell you that this is how it works for your business, based on those case studies. But the reality is that every business is different. And there are different things that occur within that specific organization. Following their recommendations is not likely to end with the best results. To get the best results in your operations, you need to intimately understand the business and the nuances of the company.

EVEN THE CONSULTING FIRMS ARE BEING DISRUPTED

The same forces of technology that put data and data analysis in easy reach of everyone are also disrupting the venerable management consulting firms. According to a 2020 white paper published by CB Insights,[1] the four functions of consulting are information, expertise, strategy, and execution. But today, "Information about customers and competitors is more available than ever. Expertise has been disaggregated. Insight has been productized (and in some cases, commoditized). And execution has, in many cases, been brought in-house or outsourced to freelancers."

It used to be that a big part of the value prop for hiring a big consulting firm was the proprietary data they had access to. They were the ones who went out and collected it. Today, you can find much of that formerly proprietary information online, or assemble it yourself with a decent CRM. Then you can use data analysis and visualization tools like PowerBI or Tableau for the insights.

The most useful insights come not from a disinterested third party who is an expert on case studies, but from someone who knows what it's like to actually work within a company and deal with the day-to-day operations. Even given the same data and the same analysis, you can be so much more effective than the big consultants because you have that intimate knowledge. And within a company, it's the accountants who should be doing the work because we already interact with other departments. And so we at least have a sense of how they already operate and understand that. Outside firms will never have that insider's perspective.

It's so easy to be a consultant and put together a presentation at the end of your engagement with the findings and suggestions and an execution plan. If you're not the person who's going to actually execute on the plan, you'll be biased in the kinds of suggestions you make, based on the outcomes of those case studies you looked at in MBA school.

IMPLEMENTATION IS THE WEAK LINK IN CHANGE MANAGEMENT

A perennial problem with execution has always been that those big firms never stick around. It might be six or 12 months after the implementation of whatever it was before you might really see if this idea worked or not. From what we've seen, it's the adoption, implementation and actual execution side that's the hardest. And you need someone there full-time to really do it.

One of the biggest jokes Mike has seen is when Peloton hired McKinsey to look at their cost structure.[2] So they paid them a huge chunk of cash to tell them they need to cut a large portion of their workforce and probably stop producing so many bikes because they're losing money. Are you really telling us that no one internally could have made that call? It is such a no-brainer. If you're concerned about spending money, don't give McKinsey a ton of money to tell you something that is just blatantly obvious. They probably had to lay off more people because they burned a bunch of cash to hire outsiders who told them something they should have been able to figure out with their own internal knowledge of the business.

When you make the decisions internally, you truly have to live with your decisions. You really have to own the changes you make, which may occur a month or two years down the road. And the true success often comes from putting manpower behind a project long-term. That's what we do here at FloQast. We don't just create a product and then move R&D on to the next one. We keep a team on that same product to keep improving it. We've found incredible success by implementing long-term strategy and not just making short-term changes, unlike Peloton, which will likely get a short-term boost from whatever McKinsey suggests, but paid a ton of money for that advice. Who won there? McKinsey doesn't have to live with it, and they don't have any long-term force behind their suggestions.

The motive for these outside firms is likely EBITDA, which doesn't necessarily correlate with building long-term value. If we brought one of those firms into FloQast, we can only imagine what their recommendations would be. They would probably tell us things like, "Stop spending so much on R&D." "This product is good enough." "Don't worry about the Customer Success team; your customers love you, so you don't need these people." "You can cut half of the company on the product side, and cut a bunch of other stuff." "By the way, you should just do a 20% across the board layoff because you can trim some fat. Do all that, and you'll get cash flow positive before you know it."

But if you look at the long-term goals we have at FloQast, we shouldn't be doing any of those things. None of those suggestions make any sense for what we are trying to do. It's a different approach and a different mentality. We can make that call internally at FloQast because we know what's going on and what our internal dynamic is. We don't need to hire someone, gather information, and then tell us to follow this same cookie-cutter model that they use as a playbook for every other company to make those companies more profitable.

A lot of times, we see companies having to use outside consultants because they have a board that doesn't trust the executive team to execute on what they're trying to do. Sometimes it's because the executive team isn't able to communicate to the board their overall intention and their plan for executing on that intention. So the board forces them to bring in consultants to validate what the executives are already working on, or to make sure that the company executes on the long-term strategy.

Another reason executives might hire those consultants is to make the difficult suggestions, especially during tough economic times like we're having now. That way, the executives can basically say, "Hey, it's not my idea, but the experts say we need to take these draconian measures to fix things." This lets them avoid responsibility for standing up there, taking responsibility and communicating their own choices to the company. So sorry, here's your email from HR, my hands were tied, but we have to do what the experts say.

In the current economic times, the easy advice is to cut, cut, and cut some more, when that's not necessarily what's right for every company. Let's take a look at a real-world example that arose during the writing of this book.

OUR RESPONSE TO THE CRUCIBLE MOMENT

In late May of 2022, Sequoia Capital released their latest doomsday slide deck, *"Adapting to Endure,"*[3] which called the current operating environment a "crucible moment." That slide deck — and the conversations around it — painted the situation as filled equally with challenges and opportunities, and recommended having plans in place to make drastic cuts if needed, especially in the areas of R&D and marketing.

But just a few days after that rather pessimistic slide deck came out, we had an all-hands meeting where we openly discussed the market and the downturn. Instead of asking consultants to come in and give us advice on what to do, we figured things out internally. Mike personally talked to all of our investors, and got a lot of different advice from them. Some were on the draconian end while others were telling us not to worry, that we would keep closing business. As a C-level team, we looked at FloQast and mapped out a strategy.

Yes, the fundraising market was tough since public markets had been crushed and VC term sheets were no longer being handed out like candy. But FloQast at that moment was sitting on a good stack of cash from previous fundraising rounds, and VC investors will still invest in great companies. Uncertainties in the world make selling a bit tougher. There was a war in Ukraine, the stock market was sliding, inflation was raging — all of which slowed buying decisions. But tech like FloQast is mission-critical. IT budgets are not being slashed, and with the ongoing talent crunch, we have strong positioning: We help accounting teams do more with less.

Our response — which we arrived at through analysis of our own conversations with team members, customers, investors, and by considering what was best for the growth of the company — was to "Play Defense but Position for Offense," as our own slide deck put it.

What did this mean? It came down to five defense tactics and seven offense tactics.

Our defense tactics:

1. Reduce our 2022 hiring plan
2. Establish a debt line
3. Scrutinize expenses more heavily
4. Implement ARR/FTE as a checking metric
5. Achieve cash flow positive in 2024, with a substantial financial backstop

And our offense tactics:

1. Adapt our positioning quickly
2. Continue to invest in go-to-market and R&D
3. Crush the Controls Workflow launch
4. Crush the Microsoft Initiative
5. Enter new territories in EMEA and Australia
6. Leverage cash reserves for opportunistic M&A
7. Push harder as a team; we will emerge victorious if we seize the moment

Now if we had hired someone like McKinsey or Bain, they almost surely would not have recommended this. They would have told us to cut nonessential marketing activities such as, for example, this book, or our investment in FloQast Studios. But at our all-hands meeting, we had an honest, non-sugar-coated discussion of the realities of the fundraising and the selling markets. Instead of an across-the-board cut — which is what outside consultants with little understanding of how FloQast operates might have suggested — Mike discussed the economic model of our business, and what the actual levers are.

Because our leadership team is heavily accountants — and heavily accountants with an operations mindset, at that — we understand how our business operates, and are not just stuck in the reporting and meaningless stats like EBITDA and viewing performance from a traditional perspective. Because we are committed to optimizing our company, and because we are focused on how our company actually works, we saw incredible opportunity in the downturn of the markets, and that this incredible opportunity will continue beyond the recovery of the markets.

Our response shows that Mike bets on his beliefs, and that FloQast as a company bets on our beliefs. We planted a flag in the ground because we believe in our systems to give us those opportunities. We're not sheltering from the storm.

So if outside consulting firms and their pricey ideas and advice aren't the way to go, who should be in charge of improving operations?

Obviously, the accountants. In this chapter, we'll explain exactly why we believe accountants should be the ones moving to lead the charge in Ops.

ACCOUNTANTS ALREADY KNOW WHAT'S GOING ON ACROSS THEIR COMPANIES

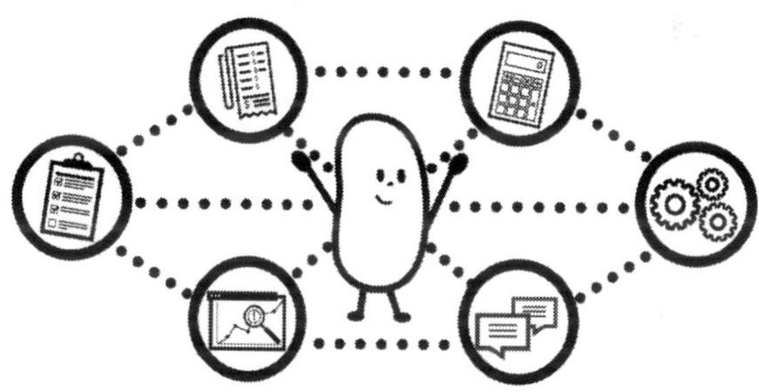

In contrast to the McKinseys and Bains and all the other big consulting firms, accountants have insanely practical, real-world experience. We can look at the big picture because of how much we already know about the business — and other businesses we worked with during our time in audit. We have in-depth experience with our organizations. We know how transactions are processed from start to end, the entire life-cycle of each number on the financials. Just about any piece of paper (or electronic file) with a number on it comes across our desk.

As Hugh O'Neill, a Chartered Accountant from Ireland who serves as a Sales Engineering Manager in the UK office, says, "If you're a controller for a business, you know how the revenue is generated, you know what the trends are, you know what's going on, you know the way to the penny from the sales team through to the payroll, and whatever is going on." Controllers and finance directors talk to people across the whole business and "everybody knows you." Besides knowing everyone, "when it comes to getting into the operations of the business, you know more than most. You're privileged to every bit of information that there is in the company, apart from some HR records and some details that may be kept away from you," Hugh said. For smaller companies, like startups, this broad knowledge across the company gives us a head start in getting into operations. You already possess "the intricate knowledge of how everything works."

Being a controller today is more than just being a number cruncher, Hugh says. "You're an accountant part of the day, you're a project manager part of the day, you're managing people part of the day, and you're managing everybody else around the organization." We have the same skills that project managers have, Hugh continued: "You do a daily standup, you list out the tasks that everybody's doing, and then you keep on top of them, you chase them. That's how you do the close."

Accounting is a cross-functional role. Besides HR, we're the only company that touches every part of a business, and we touch every part in way more depth than HR does. When

Jaysen Dyal worked at a video game company, he experienced the intense interaction with various parts of the company :

> *We had to know what the engineers were doing in order to know what to capitalize and what to expense. We had to talk to the engineers. 'What's the status of your projects?' 'Did you have any major overhauls?' 'What's on the horizon?' We had to check in with legal. 'What litigation do we have ongoing?' 'What's the status of a past legal action?' Or, 'Has this thing closed out?' 'Do we have anything coming up?' Because that all needs to be disclosed. So it's a very cross-functional role.*

Being a former pre-med student, Jaysen saw accounting as being similar to checking the vital stats of a person. Every time you go see a doctor, the first few steps are always the same. A nurse or PA will check your vitals to get an overall view of your health and get an idea of which specialist you might need to see. Similarly, every month, the accountants go through the same steps to gauge the health of a business by checking in with the different parts of the company, as Jaysen recounts: "Now from there, you might find out that engineering is starting a new project. And that's going to kick off a whole new set of steps. Because now I have to check in with them on the status of that every month."

Only accounting has its finger on the pulse of every vital sign in a company. "It surprises me that the accountants wouldn't play a much more central role in understanding the health of a business," Jaysen says. But, he adds, "it's like there's no upside, it's all downside if you're not operating efficiently. You get used to not getting much credit for when things go right. But if you can put that person in more of a central role, where things are operating efficiently and operating as they should, it becomes more like doing a good job as a referee."

Jaysen, who used to referee youth soccer, says, "You do your best job as a referee when they don't talk about you. If people don't say a word about the ref, any calls that he made, then the referee did a good job."

No other department knows as much about the details of how the company operates as accounting does. While we may not understand the precise details of how a product is developed, "we know what it takes to monitor that development, manage the transactions, book an order, ship the product and collect the cash," says Shivang Patel. "Accounting is the only department that knows how to run the business from start to finish."

Jerry Raphael, CFO of Hypori, agrees, and says "I almost hate it when they call it back office, because we're right there on the front lines, with everyone, enabling things to happen, whether it's a sale, whether it's hiring an employee, whether it's getting someone paid, or bringing on a new partner or vendor." The controller has a front seat to different things going on within the organization.

The close process is a big part of why we already know what's going on across our organizations, according to our CFO, Razzak Jallow. "The close process is the only time the whole company has to get together and is forced to agree on what happened in the prior month or the prior quarter." That forcing function around the close brings together people from different parts of the organization who have different perspectives, from pure GAAP-based rules to the internal models and rules on how we track and how we give credit for things, and all these perspectives need to be ironed out in a very short timeframe. From all these different pieces, the accountants extract the information that determines "how we view ourselves as a company, and what we need to do going forward," Razzak explains.

Our skillset as accountants, as Razzak says, "entails a deep understanding of not just the numbers, but why the numbers are the way they are, and what actually happened to get it there." That deep understanding and the ability to connect the dots in designing operations becomes crucial in making sure that a startup — which may not show a profit for 10 years — is on the right path to eventual profitability. As Razzak explains, "a million dollars in revenue is very different if it's coming from recurring revenue from a happy customer than if it's a one-time professional services piece of revenue that was outsourced, so you didn't make any money on it at all." Our skills will become ever-more valuable as emerging business models become more complex and more networked.

Accountants, besides knowing how everything works, also are a very realistic group. They've actually seen how poorly some of this stuff can go. They have experience on the ground of getting stuff done. They know what it takes to make a process change in a company. And they also have those crucial cross-functional relationships.

In contrast, when you bring in an outside consultant to make process changes, people are likely to get defensive, and see it as these outsiders telling them what they're doing wrong. Without those relationships, those outsiders are just not going to be in as good of a position to collaborate around operations and work to improve things.

But when the ideas come from accounting, they generally come across as friendly or helpful. Because you have an idea of the pressures that other parts of the company work under, you have more credibility in suggesting ideas that will work for both that area and for accounting. Others in the company see you there every day, consistently as an employee, and you're going to be there for the duration of the execution. It's one thing to work with someone from the accounting team, someone you know and trust, and who you know is working toward the same overall company goals that you are, and it's another thing entirely to work with a Harvard MBA from McKinsey. In the latter case, people are just not going to be as comfortable working with that Harvard MBA who comes in with the attitude of knowing how things should be done, based on the case studies they memorized. People will think, "What does that asshole think I'm doing wrong?" They'll feel like they're being questioned on the quality of their work. They won't be as receptive or open to a new approach.

Besides not being entirely trusted because they're outsiders, consultants lack the in-depth knowledge of how end-to-end transactions work in a company. They may have a general understanding of how the accounting cycle works, but they don't know the specifics. Those McKinsey MBAs have never actually done the work. They haven't been the boots on the ground, getting to the close every month.

Besides understanding how the business operates, as accountants, we always have in the back of our minds the data flow from transaction to financial statements. The operational accountant is, as Dante Giannini puts it, "a critical partner to the accounting side of things." You need to "support both sides of the house" so that the process works for everyone. You don't want to "throw something over the fence because you're now just crushing somebody on the other side," Dante continues, "So as we look to optimize the process all the way through, you need to think about not just what information you're getting, but where that information is going. And that's a big thing that I'm pushing everybody on, which is making sure they understand all the critical touch points beyond just themselves." While it's still OK to focus solely on the accounting as a core competency, that's a limiting perspective, according to Dante:

> *To be more than that, in today's world, you really need to understand how everything is flowing and fitting together, where your risk points are, how you address them and how you make sure that you know that everybody who's working at your company is trying to do the best they can. So how do you support them? How do you make sure that everything's good so that the work is being distributed equally and nobody's getting crushed?*

ACCOUNTANTS BRING DISCIPLINE TO THE WORK

Everyone in business recognizes that accounting is a highly successful team that works under intense pressure every day, and yet we're able to execute continuously with excellence. We operate under a cadence of closing the books every month, every quarter, and every year. That discipline of following a regular cadence can be brought to the rest of an organization. No matter what someone is doing, whether it's marketing, sales, production, or even creating new and unique deliverables, there's a cadence to what goes on. But outside of accounting, there tends to be very little sense of iterating and optimizing.

Most businesses operate in a reactive state, where they're just responding to what comes up, as it comes up, as a one-off process. But it's in the DNA of accountants to develop coherent, consistent processes and to constantly improve them and to be a catalyst for change. So when organizations allow the accounting leader to apply the discipline of operationalizing and optimizing across the organization, the business can move into a proactive state. The business is no longer a group of random individuals, but a cohesive team, working for a common goal.

That discipline accountants bring ensures consistency, as Lilith Chrakian found when she took responsibility for commissions for the sales team. While the sales team cares most about closing deals, the team managers want to make sure their reps are paid in agreement with their commission plans and paid well so that the good ones don't leave. Lilith worked with the sales team to develop a standard like set of rules, so that "every time there's something outside the box, we find a solution for it, so that we're still following the commission plan, but also in a way that's a repeatable process."

Bringing discipline and consistency to our work doesn't mean we are rigid in how we do things, as Shivang Patel cautions. "One challenge is that sometimes as an accountant we get too comfortable with 'this is how we've always done it.'" Our experiences with a broad range of scenarios mean we should know that nothing lasts forever. Businesses change, and so should our assumptions and our processes. For Shivang, it's a huge red flag, when someone calls themself an operational accountant, but leans on the process from last month, last quarter, or last year. "If we don't take a fresh look at it every month, then you're not necessarily an operational accountant, you're a walk-by accountant," says Shivang.

If you've risen to the level of controller, you're the kind of person who gets stuff done. You don't sit around. Stefan likens it to the dedication of farmers, who just get up every day and do the work. They don't wait and worry about things, but just do it. They use their energy for action, not for worrying, as Winston Churchill said: "Let our advance worrying become advanced thinking and planning." Stefan believes that controllers share a personality trait that keeps them moving forward and motivates them to help the organization. When they see that something needs to be done, they just go ahead and do it.

ACCOUNTANTS ARE TRAINED IN A CULTURE OF CONSTANT IMPROVEMENT

Another reason we think accountants should take over operations is that we work in a culture of review. We're used to having someone look at our work, while most other parts of the organization do not have a sophisticated review culture. If there is any kind of review in operations, it's generally a little toxic. When someone points out problems with processes, the response is generally not to ask for ideas on how to make it better. Instead, people tend to get defensive, and say, "No, I didn't do it wrong, there isn't a better way to do it, and this is the best way to do it."

But in accounting, our culture of review results in a less defensive mentality. That culture of review means the best idea wins, not the idea from the person with the most influence. We know that when someone's reviewing our work, they're not trying to be a jerk, but they're doing it to assist and to help. We understand that errors occur, and we want that second or third set of eyes to take a look and find those mistakes before the work goes any further. Accountants are used to having their work reviewed and critiqued to make it better.

That culture of review also is helpful for building a team, according to Lilith Chrakian, who credits the review process with helping her develop "a team of individuals who were just as detailed and good to our clients as I was. You really couldn't get away with much when I was reviewing. That translated to a whole team of individuals like that, and now they can run that team without me," she said.

One of Stefan's favorite sayings is, "Trust, but verify." That first word is key; we're not reviewing work because we're looking for problems or because we think people are lazy or doing a bad job, but because we want to be sure the work is materially correct, and is done efficiently and effectively. This is another cultural attribute we bring to the table.

When you get accountants in operations, then you have monthly and maybe even weekly feedback. You can see right away if your idea is working. You can change things on the fly when you see things aren't working, or if conditions change suddenly, as they did with the pandemic.

If you're an operations person, you're going to sit down with all the stakeholders and interview them to learn about their process. You're going to figure out what's going wrong, and where the bottlenecks are. Since our work is affected by processes across the whole organization, we actually already know where the skeletons are. We have a sense of where things are going wrong, and we can get the issues out on the table in a much friendlier and easier way. External consultants or internal ops groups might not have as much success getting those pain points out and finding ways to make things better for the whole process and, in turn, the whole organization.

ACCOUNTANTS KNOW THE VALUE OF A SINGLE SOURCE OF TRUTH

You're getting ready for a board meeting, and the sales team has revenue numbers pulled from one system, and the FP&A team has numbers from a different system, and neither of those are remotely close to what's in your ERP. Maybe it's just a few thousand, but what if the difference is millions of dollars in revenue? Then you have a massive fire drill, trying to figure out what the difference is, and wasting hours working through embarrassingly large discrepancies. Does this sound familiar?

It's high stress because it's revenue and it's for the board. The numbers have to be right. You have to make sure that everything ties out. Misspellings are not tolerated. Transposed numbers are not acceptable.

Everyone on the FloQast team who's worked in industry has horror stories like these — we're leaving out the names to protect the innocent — and even here at FloQast, it has been a journey to achieve that single source of truth. As a startup, you hack your way there. You're relying on multiple systems, but a few years ago, as we discussed way back in Chapter 1, it broke when some of our board materials did not agree. Our Customer Success team had one number, but finance had another number. It's not a good look.

When you're scaling, by the time you reach thousands of employees, and if you have any hope of having any semblance of good operations, you have to get that sorted out.

One of the first projects Adam Schall pitched when he came on board was to implement a business intelligence tool so that everyone — the board, the leadership team, and managers — can all go to one tool for their specific metrics or KPIs, and "that's the source of truth." Adam adds, "It might be pulling from different sources, but that is the governing data for the company."

No one — and especially not accountants — enjoys going through a fire drill every month to get all the siloed operations to reconcile to the same numbers, but that's the normal routine when accountants aren't overseeing operations.

Those numbers need to be owned by an independent party who does not have skin in the game. Different parts of the organization have different incentives. Marketing might want a particular lead attributed to their efforts because they need it to hit their targets. But sales might claim it because they booked that lead initially, so you get all this fighting about it. The most independent party you have at any organization is finance, so they should be the ones owning the single source of truth. They can sit in the middle as arbiters, look at the data, and decide where the lead gets attributed or what the real numbers are.

Jerry Raphael likens this to a "separation of church and state." When the sales people focus on closing deals and the accounting team is the sole source of reporting on what deals closed during the period, that brings more oversight and governance. Part of his process is to create standard definitions of metrics and the methods of calculating those metrics, plus the discipline of a review process. It makes it more difficult for anyone "to paint a rosier picture."

By bringing accountants and their discipline around the close to other company-wide reporting, everyone shares a common language and single source of truth. In Jerry's experience, at the companies where he's implemented this process, "it definitely gives you the ability to move a lot faster." Instead of spending time in conversations around "Where did this number come from?" and "What is the calculation?" and spending time on separate calculations because "I don't trust what comes out of here," the shared accountability keeps everyone on the same page and using the same information. Jerry says, "It's absolutely critical, in my opinion, to companies being able to succeed."

ACCOUNTING IS THE LANGUAGE OF BUSINESS

During an interview with CNBC, Warren Buffett said "Accounting is the language of business," as a reminder that if you want to truly understand what is going on in businesses as an investor, you need to understand accounting.

Perhaps not so famously, Mike said "Operations is the playbook for how to run your business."

Besides being the language of business, accounting also is the historian of business. There's that old saying from Winston Churchill: "Those that fail to learn from history are doomed to repeat it." Our most basic work product is acting as historians for our businesses to produce financial statements and footnotes, which are the most important output for investors and all the other stakeholders. That historical focus of accounting forms a big part of our coursework and a massive part of the CPA exam.

The external users — the bankers and investors — rely on the accounting being done correctly and in compliance with GAAP. The power of GAAP is that it's generally accepted. The rules are the rules. Following GAAP, we translate the events that happen in a company and translate them into a universal language in number form. Then, to help the users of those financials understand what happened, we translate those numbers into words for the footnotes.

It's not just the numbers and the formatting of financials that are important in our work. It's also the words that are in the notes. It's knowing what people care about, and explaining it clearly. For example, within a 10Q and a 10K, you need to be able to explain the year-over-year changes percentage wise, as well as point out the business reasons for those changes.

With GAAP, everyone is on the same page, so it's possible to do an apples-to-apples analysis of publicly traded companies. An investor who's trying to decide whether to invest in tech or consumer products or oil and gas doesn't need to understand the details of how all of those companies make money in their very different ways. They don't need to be an expert in each industry to be able to decide which one to invest in. GAAP makes it possible for an average person to understand the financials. The bankers and investors need to know if a business and its operations fits within their risk profile.

Those financials are the starting point not only for external reporting, but also for internal decision-making. As CEO of a company, Mike now relies on regular reports to see how we're doing against our goals. But like many CEOs, he doesn't rely on

GAAP financials to make decisions. He doesn't worry about things like EBITDA or gross margin; those are under the purview of our most excellent CFO.

Internally, we use SaaS metrics. We look at metrics like "How much cash do we have? What is our burn rate? What was our efficiency last quarter?" Mike's main focus is on making a great product and serving our customers. "I would hope that most CEOs aren't sitting there freaking out about optimizing gross margin, but that they're thinking bigger picture and longer term," Mike says. But while SaaS metrics are a great tool for internal reporting, the problem is there's no generally accepted methodology for calculating things like NRR, or net recurring revenue, so investors can't rely on those metrics unless they can audit the numbers effectively.

After you've worked a few years as an accountant, you get a sense of the relationships between accounts, and can spot when something is off from a mile away. As Jaysen Dyal says in some simple examples, "You know the change in accumulated depreciation should equal your depreciation expense, minus any sales of fixed assets. For a SaaS company, the gross decrease in deferred revenue should equal the increase in revenue." The operational accountant takes that understanding from the financials to operations, as Jaysen continues, "So if this is how it's going in engineering, how does that affect something else in your organization? It's just converting from numbers to operations."

Operational accountants develop an understanding of how transactions flow from point of origin to the report. That understanding helps you decide on your processes. If you don't set that at the point of transaction correctly, you might have an unfavorable outcome from sending that process that way. So you really want someone who understands the language to make sure the transaction translates correctly.

You also want someone who understands how the design of business processes can determine how transactions show up in the financials, according to Razzak Jallow, CFO of FloQast. Although most accounting regulations are black and white, there are some gray areas in there. "Accountants are well-positioned to figure out the signal to noise ratio and help guide the company on when we should build our processes around how it will show up in the P&L, say, under ASC 606, and when we should build our processes around the underlying value to the customer, and live with the noise in the P&L," says Razzak, adding that "those questions are always interesting to tackle."

Here's a little anecdote from FloQast about how GAAP can drive business decisions. Under EITF 08-1, you have to recognize implementation revenue over the lifetime of a customer, which is around nine years for us. So we were having a discussion around giving away our implementations for free, and deploying that as a weapon in the market for winning more deals. Mike was in the room and realized that if we did that, we would accelerate our revenue recognition. We would be discounting less on the software side — which gets recognized over three years — and we wouldn't be putting anything in the nine-year bucket.

It was odd that this decision that would hurt us from a cash flow perspective and a margin perspective was actually beneficial for us from a GAAP perspective, because our recognition period would be shorter. Having Mike in the room so he could explain how that decision would ultimately flow to the financials was really helpful for leadership in making that call. Generally, something that sales wants to do is at odds with what's going to present well in the financials. But this was one of those instances where both aligned really well.

SOX 404 POSITIONED US TO MOVE INTO OPERATIONS

It's not often that the regulatory environment actually helps us to move into the future rather than dragging us down, but that's what happened when Sarbanes-Oxley was passed in 2002. SOX 404 requires that every process with a control risk behind it (and almost every process has a control risk behind it) and every process that touches the financials (and every process touches the financials somehow) has to be documented.

Mike joined public accounting as all of the public companies were going through all their first SOX audits. He remembers it as a fascinating time:

> *The billable hours were through the roof, and everyone was trying to figure out what* SOX *meant, how to implement it, and how to document processes at the same time. I was watching the transition from balance sheet audits into control-based audits in real time. And the amount of challenge people were having just simply writing all this stuff down was mind-boggling to watch. Initially, that was prepared by the accounting staff in conjunction with the auditors.*
>
> *At first, we prepared these long Word documents called narratives or walk-throughs as the starting point for all of this. We would sit down with someone in accounting and have*

them walk through in excruciating detail exactly how they did their jobs, everything from entering the password to log into NetSuite, and what the password requirements were, to the tab someone clicked on with a screenshot of that tab. But after the SEC complained that those narratives often had holes in them because the people writing them down didn't really understand the processes, people started doing them in flowcharts.

It was a very collaborative process back then, between accountants and auditors. These days, the accounting department should be the ones putting it together and the auditor should just be reviewing it.

SOX forced accountants and auditors to look closely at the operations of businesses, which puts accountants — and the auditors who will eventually move into industry — in the perfect position to move into operations. Without SOX, we don't think accountants would be as operational as we are today. It's sort of an unnatural thing that these onerous laws have actually set in motion the changes we have needed to move in the direction of the future.

Oh, and that extra scrutiny is not going away. Between the SEC and the PCAOB, nothing has ever happened to suggest that there will ever be less scrutiny, less documentation, less proof that the accounting and the business processes are operating properly.

BRING THE DNA AND CULTURE OF ACCOUNTING TO THE BROADER ORGANIZATION

Throughout this chapter, we've pointed out the characteristics of accountants that make us perfectly suited to bring an operational approach to our companies. We're not saying that accounting should run the world, but rather that bringing the way we run ourselves, the skills and knowledge we already have, and the rigor we demonstrate to the broader organization can't help but make our organizations better. In the next chapter, we'll look at the advantages of moving into the operational approach for both the organization and the individual accountant.

6 / ADVANTAGES OF MOVING INTO AN OPERATIONAL APPROACH

THE ONE QUESTION everyone has (or should have) before making any significant change is "What's in it for me?" Most people don't willingly make huge changes in how they do their jobs if there's no upside. So what's the upside for organizations and for accountants who take on a more operational approach?

TRANSFORMING ACCOUNTING FROM A COST CENTER TO A PROFIT DRIVER

The biggest priority for controllers and CFOs is ensuring that their company will be around to take on the challenges of tomorrow, whatever those challenges may be. The businesses that succeed are those that are in a perpetual state of improvement.

As we discussed in Chapter 3, operationalizing your company is measuring the abstract and tracking it with the intention of making it better. The Ops approach means you're using tech and machines to do what they do best, so that your employees become strategic assets and can do what humans do best, which is solving problems creatively. You're getting the highest and best use out of all your employees.

Companies that embrace change culture and are capitalizing on the abilities of their team members are inherently more agile. Perpetual improvement keeps you on the cutting edge, and able to adjust quickly to any situation that comes your way.

Operationalizing your department, your company, and the way you do business will improve your company's performance the same way that consistent exercise and practice makes you a better performer as a human.

An operational approach also means that once the menial tasks are automated, your team has the bandwidth to take on higher order work. Jaysen Dyal says this means you can be "part of the business decisions that are being made." For example, the engineers might have questions about whether to outsource part of a project, or to build it in-house, or about how many engineers to hire. "And those questions are all going to get answered by accountants," Jaysen continued. "They'll be able to say 'Here's how the numbers look when we outsource it, and here's how the numbers look if we develop it in-house. Here's how the numbers work if we put five engineers on the project, and it takes longer, versus throwing 10 people at it and we get it done in a shorter time.'" These are the more interesting projects, and this work can make a direct contribution to the company's bottom line.

The Ops approach can also help keep everyone aligned with the same incentives, as FloQast CFO Razzak Jallow explains. "A huge risk for every company is when there's disconnectedness and one team is actually rowing in a slightly different direction than what the company needed." This can be very painful for organizations when there's a disconnect between team goals and overall company strategy. "Accounting sees the end numbers for the company, and is well-positioned to bring insights on where goals or actions are actually working for the company or against the company." With the Ops mentality, when all pieces of the organization are connected, everyone is rowing together in the same direction and at the same speed.

ACCOUNTING IS FUN AGAIN

A tight talent market combined with the Great Reshuffling means it's super critical to keep your best people. An Ops approach means the accounting team becomes less of a cost center and more of a strategic asset. Your people are more able to do work that matters and that makes a difference in their organizations, instead of feeling like a cog in a giant machine. They're not siloed off with the mundane and repetitive, but instead they collaborate across the company to do the more fun work that stretches them out of the box of debits and credits. They become problem solvers. And all of that makes it more likely that they'd rather stay at the exciting and engaging company than work for the dull competitor.

Our research for the Controller's Guidebook backs this up. When we asked accountants about their level of fulfillment at work and their likelihood of staying with their current employer, we found that people were much more likely to stay when work was fulfilling.[1] Accountants with a high degree of fulfillment were five times more likely to stay than when their fulfillment was just average, and 12 times more likely than someone with low fulfillment. The Ops approach is all about contributing more to your workplace than just adding numbers to reports; it's about making the workplace better for everyone.

Ultimately, this may make accounting more attractive for young people. Younger people crave work that helps them contribute to something bigger than themselves. And with an operational approach, our controller Greg Vecellio says "people will see that there's a bigger purpose" to their work. Instead of being chained to a computer in a row of cubicles, Greg says the new image of accounting will be that they're "actually going to be out there doing things, talking to people, working on projects cross functionally," which will make operational accounting a highly desirable career path. The skills and experience gained from an operational role can be further leveraged to whole new roles within the accounting function, or across different business functions to provide, as Greg says, "limitless opportunities."

Younger accountants clearly crave this variety. Greg says that when people from other parts of the organization come to accounting for help on a project, he can always find volunteers among his younger team members, even if the extra project adds to their workload. "Nobody's ever pushed back and said, 'I'm too busy. I don't want to do that.' It gives them a spark." These extra projects provide the kind of growth challenge younger accountants seek out to keep their work fresh and exciting, and are a nice break from doing journal entries.

As we mentioned in the introduction, there are organizations out there that have figured out how to make accounting a fulfilling and rewarding career. When we did our survey for Chapter 4 of the Controller's Guidebook: When Accountants

Dare to Dream, 15% of our respondents rated their level of fulfillment at the A-level, and another 5% gave their workplace fulfillment level an A+.[2] So while this isn't *all* the organizations, and while 15% gave their workplace fulfillment a failing grade, this means that what we're saying in this book is achievable with today's technology. You don't have to wait for the next revolutionary piece of software to have a great experience at work.

DO MORE WITH FEWER PEOPLE

For basically longer than we've been alive, accounting departments have been understaffed. But with the Ops approach (and implementing tech like FloQast), it's possible to streamline close processes to operate with fairly lean teams, as Jonathan Hardy found at LeadVenture. His team shaved 15 days off the close, going from 20 days to just five days while adding just one or two people to an understaffed team. "There's a lot of processes and systems that changed to get there outside of just adding heads," he said. "Because throwing bodies at a problem doesn't always solve the problem." We couldn't agree more.

LESS RISK, MORE ACCURATE NUMBERS

Besides not having the issues we described earlier in Chapter 4, where we looked at the symptoms of organizations that need an operational approach, you'll have better, more accurate numbers. As Hugh O'Neill puts it, "There's a level of checking the numbers that comes with the mechanics of checking the numbers, and then there's the level of checking the numbers that comes with knowing what is going on and being tuned into operations."

For example, when everyone suddenly went remote during

COVID, Hugh says that payroll became more difficult because you didn't see people around the office, and it became harder to track "who's coming, who's going, and the smell test. If you don't know the details of what you're doing and what you're reviewing, you can miss stuff, because it can be a very mechanical transaction. Whereas, the more depth and knowledge of the business you have," the better you're able to connect what's happening in the business to what shows up in the financials, Hugh says. "But if you don't have your finger on the pulse of what's going on in the business, then you're no good to nobody."

By applying the Ops approach when he was Director of Accounting Initiatives at LeadVenture, Jonathan Hardy's team had more confidence in their numbers from a control standpoint "because they know what they're doing." When the FP&A team asked about changes in revenue or costs, "we were able to provide answers because we were not just doing — we were actually trying to understand it at the same time." The additional time gained from streamlining processes meant that Jonathan could spend more time thinking about what he was doing instead of worrying about whether he remembered everything.

A common headache for accounting is having to fix the things that come into the GL wrong. When Greg Vecellio, our controller here at FloQast, got "away from the pure transactional mentality" in a previous position by spending time away from his desk and with people out at various sites "where the work was actually being done," he saw those kinds of problems. He would ask people, "Did you realize this causes a problem on the backend, and that there are downstream impacts that somebody will have to go in and fix?" At first, he would get mad, but then he realized that people really didn't know, and that they were just doing their jobs the way they were trained. "It was really eye-opening to see the work through somebody else's lens. It opens up your mind," he said. Through those conversations with people in other parts of the organization, he's been able to solve problems at their source, reducing the amount of re-work needed downstream, and having more fun at the same time. "I thrive on helping others solve problems," Greg said. "This approach has carried forward to help me be more outward-looking than inward-looking," he concludes.

CAREER AND PROFILE BOOST WITHIN YOUR COMPANY

If you've gotten this far in our book, chances are you're not one of those accountants who's content with the status quo and with just drifting along through life. Instead, we're pretty sure you're looking for ways to chart a path to a more strategic and less tactical career. So taking an operational role can be, in Shivang Patel's words, "the fastest way to accelerate your career growth" as well as "pretty exciting." This comes from focusing "on how I can best understand my role, the role of those around me, and connecting those operational dots." Based on Shivang's own experience, accountants who take on an operational role have a clear path up the career ladder for promotions while picking up valuable skill sets.

As the "SAP guy" at Ruckus Wireless, Shivang had people come to him for help who would never have spoken to him otherwise, including the CEO who needed help with invoicing. He had conversations with the general counsel, who needed his advice in a lawsuit. He also was called upon to lead training sessions across the company and around the world, experiences he never thought he would have had back in his days in audit.

For Shivang, while the company-wide recognition of his skills as the "SAP guy" surely raised his profile, he received perhaps more satisfaction from "being given a problem, figuring it out, and then helping someone. The look on their face and the excitement they had when something worked, and knowing it was his knowledge and direction that allowed them to figure out the solution; that was priceless."

Jonathan Hardy also says his unique skill set as an operational accountant has helped him progress quickly, especially "for how short my career has been so far." Even though he only got his bachelor's in accounting in 2013, in 2019, he was hired as assistant controller at LeadVenture. Two years later, he was promoted to Director of Accounting Initiatives, and in 2023, he moved over to Director of Special Projects. His current position, still at LeadVenture, is Director of FP&A.

Embracing the Ops mindset of "wanting to know more and wanting to understand it, and then taking the initiative to do it" sets Jonathan apart from the majority of accountants he's worked with who focus more on the sequence of processes and tie-outs they need to complete. "The Ops mindset has separated me from a lot of my peers, because they don't think that way," he says. "Opportunities have come up because I can think outside of the box, and outside of an Excel file with the debits and credits."

Jerry Raphael, CFO of Hypori, found that learning about how the business operated helped move his career forward, because he was able to talk to leaders about the things they cared about. "I couldn't go to some of these more senior leaders and talk about accruals and journal entries and reconciliations. That's not the way business leaders speak," he said. "If you're stuck in the world of accounting and just talking the jargon we know as CPAs or as controllers, you will always be stuck."

But as Jerry learned about how the company made money, who the target customer was, how the sales department was organized and compensated, and what the leading indicators for the business were, as well as industry best practices, he was able to move his career forward quickly. "Those are the types of topics that folks will talk to you about on a regular basis," he said. "It's really about how we're going to move forward, from a sales perspective, or product perspective, or even an employee headcount perspective, to get things done."

MOVING YOUR ORGANIZATION FORWARD WITH THE OPS APPROACH

Being operationally sound gives you more time to pick your head up and improve. It prevents you from being what looks like a calm duck on the surface, while your feet are actually paddling like mad underwater. It gives you the time to move forward in a progressive organization. The more opportunity you have to look at technology and improvement, the better. With the development of AI and deep learning models, you will have an opportunity to look at things in a way that can be more powerful than what we have today. The accounting knowledge — the people, the workflow, the data, the numbers and what the outputs will be — still puts you in the best position to help make IT-related decisions and understand how thing should work and how you can best automate the upfront effort to make sure you're getting the appropriate data on the back end.

The Ops approach isn't just about the physical things you do at the workplace to get the work done. It's not just leveraging technology to smooth out workflows, eliminate bottlenecks, and enhance the flow of data to get the reporting done more efficiently and accurately. As we mentioned in Chapter 3, the Ops approach also is a mindset shift. You're shifting your thinking from focusing on the past, to thinking about how the upstream activities impact the data that emerges at the end. You're deepening your understanding of how the entire organization functions, and you're expanding the sphere of your knowledge and influence. This expansion in your thinking also will enable you to solve two of the biggest intangible issues that every organization faces: the problems of perception and communication, which will be the focus of the next chapter.

7 / HOW THE OPS APPROACH SOLVES THE TWO BIGGEST ISSUES OF EVERY BUSINESS

Good communication is the bridge between confusion and clarity.
—*Nat Turner*

Perception is reality. If you are perceived to be something, you might as well be it because that's the truth in people's minds.
—*Steve Young*

Before we get into how you actually move into an Ops role, let's take a step back and talk about how Ops can help with the two biggest issues in business. Every company will have problems along the way. It's part of the normal life cycle of every business. But Stefan believes — and this is the hill he'll die on

— that the two biggest issues that companies struggle with are communication and perception.

Organizations have a hard time communicating, mainly because people tend to be bad at communicating with each other. Communication problems can be as simple as "Is this ready? Is this good to go?" They also show up as poor instructions about how to do certain things, or uncertainty about what's happening across the organization, or about the overall goals a company is trying to accomplish. Some people might not be getting the message because it's not coming across in their preferred means of communication.

Another common issue with communication is translating spoken word explanations into written process documentation. When you hear and see someone speaking, besides the words, you also get their body language, gestures, tone, eye contact and facial expressions, all of which can communicate volumes more than the actual words being spoken. This means that when you use tech to communicate, you need to be cognizant of the context that may be needed to avoid miscommunication.

This extra context from nonverbal communication can be either good or bad, depending on the situation. For example, if someone texts you or Slacks you that they need you to do something, it might cause you extra stress if the priority of the new assignment isn't included in the message. This can cause extra stress if you think you need to drop everything (potentially including family priorities) to get this done immediately, when that was not the intent of the requester.

On the other hand, stripping out the emotional context that might come from a verbal message from someone who's having a bad day for unrelated reasons will notify you of the assignment you now have, but not cause you to second-guess about the reason for their bad mood.

While emotional intelligence is an essential part of communication and perception, there can be too many opportunities for others to misread or misunderstand your intent. If all parties can agree to remove the emotion from lines of communication, discussions can be more effective and less ambiguous. It can be a more pure form of communication. While you might disagree about the process or the priorities, at least you're not confused about the ask or what's being communicated.

Because we tend to be bad at communicating with each other, organizations and the people in them have a hard time with perception around their companies.

We accountants tend to have weird perceptions of what sales does, and the folks in sales likewise have weird perceptions of what accounting does. So we find it hard to communicate with each other, which doesn't do anything to correct the weird perceptions we have of what the other areas of the company do. Because we don't understand what other people do, we don't know what they might need from accounting or other parts of the company that would make their jobs easier. There's a lack of clarity around who needs what, why they need it, when they need it, and where they can find this information.

Communication and perception problems often surface during the execution of a plan. People figure out their role, but what they struggle with is not knowing which person has been charged with a specific piece of the plan, or that someone in another part of the organization could help them with an assigned task. So, almost inevitably, communication breaks down, and people give up on the new plan. Everyone goes back to their regular tasks and their regular way of doing things.

But when you have better perception and communication, people generally figure things out. They know who can help them, and who's doing what. There might be 1,000 ways to get the work done, and together, they're able to figure out which one will actually work and they're smart enough to handle execution on that chosen path.

COMMUNICATION PROBLEMS ARE EVERYWHERE

Although 93% of business leaders say "communication is the backbone of business," we don't always do it right, according to a survey by Grammarly.[1] That same survey found that most knowledge workers, including people in finance and accounting, spend about half the week on writing tasks. A whopping 86% of those who spent that much time writing reported communication issues. So your company is not alone if you have communication issues.

Those problems in communication can be costly; Grammarly estimated the total cost of ineffective communication among knowledge workers in the U.S. could be as high as $1.2 trillion per year. That comes out to $625,300 per year for companies with 500 or more employees. Ouch.

Communication problems aren't just a bottom line issue. They also impact leadership. Researchers at Stanford[2] analyzed comments on leadership assessments and found that leaders are 10 times more likely to be criticized for under-communication as for overcommunication. That same study also found that leaders who under-communicate are viewed as less qualified for their leadership role.

Even McKinsey has noted communication problems. Although we think they're terrible as business consultants, they're not so bad when they stick to research. A recent McKinsey report[3] blamed communication issues as one of the contributing factors to the Great Resignation, when 19 million knowledge workers left their jobs. They found that 54% of knowledge workers and 79% of business leaders experience miscommunication at least weekly.

This can be disastrous for companies because, as the report said, "First, conveying information accurately and efficiently is essential to business operations. Second, knowledge workers and business leaders spend a significant amount of the workweek in communication." So if we're communicating poorly, we're wasting a good chunk of our time, instead of doing things that move the organization toward its goals. That wasted time and effort — especially in the startup community — can translate to business failure and to investors pulling their support.

PERCEPTION REQUIRES A DEEP, WIDE ANGLE VIEW

Perception is more than seeing what's going on in your organization. Perception is moving a step beyond the sensory and information input to understand what's happening at a deep level. It's a deep, wide angle view. But because all of us come to our work with different frameworks of understanding, we will all perceive the same situation differently.

An esoteric way to understand perception is to think about Plato's allegory of the cave, where a group of prisoners have spent their lives, chained so they face a blank wall. All they see are shadows projected from objects or puppets passing in front of a fire behind them. This is their entire view of reality. But in an organization, it's often like everyone has their own cave, and everyone is seeing a different set of shadows, completely unaware that they have a different understanding of what the reality is.

If you bind yourself to your own view of reality and are unwilling to broaden that view, you will most likely have a hard time working well with others. You come away with a distorted awareness of how the different parts and the individual contributors of an organization work together — or rather, how they aren't working well together, at least not according to your limited view of the shadows on your cave wall.

An example of this distorted view of reality is that most accountants have a limited understanding of marketing. Their perception of marketing is that these people are lazy and aren't doing any hard work to justify all the money they spend. And perception is a two-way street: Many people in other parts of the organization don't realize all the ways they can work with and collaborate with accounting and finance. Their perception of us as demanding and unhelpful overrides reality. They tend to see us as the office of No.

Another way that perception issues surface in organizations is in lack of clarity about individual roles. A lack of role clarity has been cited in research by Gallup as one of the main causes of burnout.[4] According to a recent Gallup State of the American Workplace report, only 60% of workers strongly agreed that they know what's expected of them at work.

Perception in business is sometimes called "organizational awareness." According to Daniel Goleman, who wrote a book on this topic, organizational awareness includes the ability to "sense the personal networks that make the organization run, and know how to find the right person to make key decisions and how to form a coalition to get something done."[5] This kind of perception is the understanding of where you fit in the grand scheme of things, and where others in the organization fit, and what everyone does. If you're able to do that, you can see where the leverage points are, and act accordingly. Without this organizational level perception, then you either succeed through serendipitous luck, or you're fighting against a machine, and you'll be inappropriately leveraged.

SOLVE BOTH PROBLEMS AT ONCE

The funny thing about the majority of these perception problems is that the fix is really simple: communication. Instead of assuming you know what someone can or can't help you with, try simply asking them. Talk to other people about what they do. We can only correct our perceptions and our understanding of others by discussion. Discussion is the first step to breaking down barriers so we can work with others more effectively, instead of just assuming we understand what their role is and how they should do their work.

We get so caught up in our own objectives that we have a limited perception of what other people do. We don't take the time to understand how other people's efforts fit into the overall picture and how we all need to work together to create something.

While accounting is the language of business, this is a language that few in our organizations outside of accounting and finance understand. What good is a language if no one understands what we are trying to communicate? We need to be better at translating and communicating what we need and what we do in terms that non-accountants can understand. This failure to translate is why perception issues often surface as communication issues.

And although accounting is the language of business, it doesn't tell the whole story. Because we as accountants understand the language of accounting, we can get caught up in the numbers as the entirety of the truth. Just as written communication strips out the body language and the nonverbal cues needed to fully grasp someone's message, the numbers strip out the story that goes with the financials. That's why we also have notes to the financials. That's why we have the Management Discussion and Analysis section, and that's why we need KPIs and metrics. A good chunk of the information that leadership needs for making decisions is not found in the income statement or balance sheet or the statement of cash flows. Our leaders and stakeholders need the stories that put those numbers in context to provide additional guidance for decisions. That's why we have slide decks for board presentations. And that's why board meetings include a lot of discussion.

The skills of communication and perception are not really something that's taught well in schools or universities, so you can pretty safely just assume that people don't have those skills. And most workplaces don't really provide their people with tools to compensate for that lack of ability.

HOW DOES AN OPS APPROACH HELP WITH THESE PROBLEMS?

Accounting and reporting are meant to improve the key issues of perception and communication within businesses. They help perception by helping others understand what the business is doing, the impacts it has, and what's driving the results. The basis of reporting is communicating the results of the cumulative effect of everyone's actions, and whether the company is meeting its goals or not.

Operational accounting starts by building bridges between accounting and the rest of your organization. It clarifies roles so people know who's responsible for what. You reduce silos so people can collaborate across the organization. As Ops begins to break down those barriers between accounting and the rest of the organization, you realize that you can interact with and work with teams in different parts of the organization in ways that help everyone. And by demonstrating your willingness to work with them, you deepen their perception of what accounting does.

It helps you build a framework of understanding to support development of a broad and deep perception of what's happening across your organization. Once you build that framework of improved perception and communication between accounting and the rest of your organization, it's easy to expand that framework across the broader organization. If you can do things to improve perception so it's more accurate, and ease communication between different areas, we believe that most companies will see a lot of issues just disappear.

Developing that broad and deep perception can make you more valuable to your organization — and to other organizations in the future. There's a reason organizations pay so much money to get people who have that wide perception and broad understanding of businesses, and that's because this is hard to develop. Those rare people who have that perception and the ability to communicate clearly across a business tend to be the most impactful.

Accounting is really just a communication tool to facilitate better decision-making. So while we may be gathering data, it's not just to hold that data. It's also to provide others with the data that impacts their work and that impacts the trajectory of the entire organization.

The reporting we do for other parts of the organization isn't just for the sake of reporting, but to help others understand what occurred and which things went well or where things went wrong — all with the end goal of helping people do their jobs better. Sometimes accountants fall into the routine of just following the reporting that was done previously. But that reporting might not be what the other people need.

So, for example, we collect data from sales, and we send them a report. But that report isn't useful unless the data has been transformed into information they can use. What would be useful is information that helps them sell better. We can't just assume we know what they need. We need to take the time to understand what information they need to influence their deals and influence their decision-making.

The Ops approach also is about taking the information from those discussions with others and translating it into standard processes and workflows. Documenting those processes in detail and agreeing to them is an essential part of optimizing operations. The spoken word isn't always the most effective means of communication. Think of the game of telephone, where the initial word or phrase has little relation to what emerges at the end. By documenting it, other people (not just the two or three involved in the initial discussion) can go back to it, see it, and understand it. You don't have to have the same conversation a thousand times. Everyone can be on the same page.

Operational accounting is a paradigm shift around the way controllers approach their organizations and the accounting function. Leveraging tech to do your work also means that the emotional intelligence aspects of communication and perception are stripped out, which also is a way of leveling the field. Operational accounting should not be something restricted to a select group of people who are inherently great at reading people and communicating. Many of us who have come up in accounting are not, and we, both Mike and Stefan, believe strongly that you don't need to possess superior emotional intelligence to excel as operational accountants. We want to build a world where everyone can do this.

Now since we all want to make a better world, in the next section of the book, we'll be talking about what you need to do to move into Ops.

PART 2

HOW TO MOVE INTO AN OPERATIONAL APPROACH

8 / WHAT SKILLS DO ACCOUNTANTS NEED TO DEVELOP FOR THE OPERATIONAL ROLE?

If you want to go fast, go alone. If you want to go far, go together.
—African proverb

BEFORE WE GET into the skills an operational accountant needs, let's talk about the position of controller for a minute. Controller is a very weird title. No other department has someone with that title. So how high-ranking do we consider the controller?

Mike has asked a lot of CFOs about this. "Every department has a VP. There's a VP of Finance, a VP of Sales, a VP of Marketing and so on, but no VP of Accounting. Instead, there's a controller. So what level do you think a controller is?" And every one of them said that the controller is a VP in their mind, a sign of how important a role controllers play.

So if that's true, then you should feel comfortable calling meetings with VPs around the organization and getting to know them a little better. But it seems like a lot of controllers don't see themselves at that level. In our conversations with controllers, most of them don't really get how important they are. So they're not going to reach out to the VP of Sales or the VP of Marketing.

And that's a mistake.

If CFOs see controllers as the equivalent of a vice president, that's the kind of clout you have — and should be willing to exercise. So, call meetings with the other VPs and get to know them. Start building relationships well before you start working on anything cross-functionally. Those relationships will help you with any future initiative you have with them. Take them to lunch, have coffee, or grab a drink. Do whatever you need to do to build those relationships. And then that will make you more effective in working with them in the future.

Now Mike can step off his soapbox and on to the skills you need for taking on an operational role. The good news is that you already have the baseline skills and knowledge, as we discussed last chapter, and the additional needs are very learnable.

We can bucket the skills you need into three areas: technology, relationships, and execution.

TECHNOLOGY

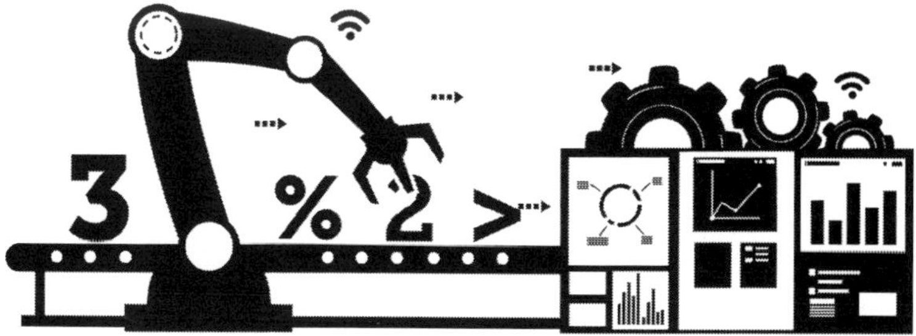

As we keep saying, there will never be enough people in accounting to get all the work done. That means using technology to automate as much as possible and to make the work for the accounting team easier will absolutely be key.

Without automation, accountants have no possibility of having any kind of reasonable life or even the mental bandwidth to take on an operational role. When we surveyed controllers in 2021,[1] one of our respondents recommended "finding systems to automate as many of your accounting tasks as possible, freeing up your time to manage, make decisions, and train as top priorities. You can't do it all, so relying on technology to free up your plate should be top of mind."

Besides automating the work, from our research for Chapter 2 of the Controller's Guidebook, "Is Your Relationship with Technology a Solution to Burnout or a Source of Stress?"[2] another key is having an integrated technology solution. Throughout this book, we've been making the case for working with an **integrated technology solution,** which we define as a tech platform that integrates all the functions and modules for accounting from ERPs to your cloud storage, and to productivity tools like Excel, to communications tools like email and Slack into a seamless workplace. Integrated tech solutions are designed to work in the ways accountants work, meeting you where you are and working the way you think and how you do your work. The tech is not merely a tool to do your job, but acts as more of a partner to help you do your job better.

However, most accountants are not so lucky. Even today, many still work with software that's largely not integrated, making the job of getting the numbers out even more painful than it needs to be. A step up above that is an **integrated technology system**, which is where most organizations exist today. While these systems may be well integrated, those integrations tend to be based pretty much solely on IT requirements, and not necessarily what the users need, nor on the downstream impacts. The emphasis is on how well the tech performs, and not on how well the user performs when they use the software. Instead of a partnership, users tend to have a fairly transactional relationship with it.

While this is obviously better than a completely unintegrated set of tools, many accountants are frustrated when they work with integrated tech systems, because they can see how close they are to the holy grail of an accounting solution that enables them to work the way they want to work.

As we'll cover more in Chapter 10, controllers and accounting teams who are fortunate to work with integrated tech solutions and who have a synergistic relationship with that tech tend to have less burnout, better work-life balance, and tend to stay with their current employer longer.

Now we realize that many controllers may have inherited workbooks or processes or tools that force you to do a lot of workarounds. Maybe the workbook was poorly designed. Or maybe the way the tool was implemented isn't optimal. And maybe your hands are tied so you can't switch out this poorly performing tool for the one you used at your last job that was so much better. Or maybe you're just not as tech savvy as you'd like to be.

Within all these parameters, we encourage accountants to step up their technology skills and find ways to make that workbook or process better. To be a strong operational accountant, our Senior Director, Growth and Strategic Initiatives, Shivang Patel, says that for an accountant to be operationally strong, you need to "understand not just how do I use the system for my role, but how can I maximize this system for the roles around me as well?" He acknowledges that some people may be more willing and able to tinker with a system and to explore all its capabilities, but to be a good operational accountant, Shivang says you've just got "to get over that hump" so you can "recommend the right efficient processes" that help everyone else do their jobs.

For example, if you're a GL accountant, and you'll need some accruals for month-end from the AP accountant, Shivang recommends working with custom reports to develop one that would enable the AP accountant to get you those accruals in a matter of minutes or hours instead of days. "If you take the initiative to go above and beyond, that helps so many others. That is a great example of a good operational accountant that can make a large impact," Shivang concluded.

Besides becoming more tech savvy, see if you can change the narrative around how you and your team interact with that technology or that workbook. Approach the work the way Lionel Messi sees the field, the players, and the ball. What can you do to reduce the friction between the work that has to get done and the people doing the work? Technology is here to make your job easier, not harder. Sometimes it just takes getting used to how that tech works and learning to think the way it thinks.

Some readers may be saying to themselves "I'm already making my ERP best in class. I'm using all the automations I can." And we say, "Great! Keep doing that!" But transactional management is only one piece of the puzzle. Now keep in mind that it's not enough to just optimize transactional management. You've also got to optimize workflow management.

That's one of the conclusions that came out of a study we did with Ventana Research looking at the impact of technology on accelerating the close, especially in the post-pandemic era.[3] We found that 54% of companies that use software to manage and automate the close process were able to complete their quarterly close within six days, while only 21% of companies that use only some workflow automations or none at all were able to close that quickly.

Those systems for automating your work are changing rapidly, so we're not going into specifics here. Any recommendations we would have — save perhaps for trying out FloQast — are likely to be outdated by the time you read this book. But we will encourage you to never completely write off something that you looked at and rejected in the past. As we know first-hand, tech companies are always adding new features and new products, so maybe this latest iteration will have all the features you need.

Controllers have a big say in the choice of accounting tech because they own the ERP, so they're going to have a say in other software that's going to be used by accounting and finance. What payroll are we going to go with? What expense system is best for us? What will we use for commissions? About the only piece they don't have much say in is the choice of CRM, because that's typically decided before the ERP is chosen. But pretty much the rest of the stack has to be approved by the controller, because it integrates with the ERP.

To be good at your job today, you need to be knowledgeable about software and IT, and you've got to understand how different apps feed into the ERP, according to Hugh O'Neill, a Chartered Accountant from Ireland who serves as Sales Engineering Manager in our U.K. office. He thinks that within 10 years, the profession will look fundamentally different, especially in the areas of payroll, AP, and AR where systems haven't yet caught up to each other to integrate. "Give it a few years and somebody will figure out ways to automate it and to make that process easier," says Hugh.

Obviously, cloud-based tools should be the first choice, not only because of the flexibility to work from anywhere, but also because that's where the future of accounting tech lies, at least until something better comes along. For collaboration with your team and with the rest of the organization, try to pick just one tool, whether it's Slack, Teams, email, or whatever the company prefers. Develop and follow company protocol in using that so that no one feels compelled to respond to messages sent at odd hours, particularly if you have team members spread across the globe, as we do at FloQast.

You also need to be constantly learning and embracing what's new. Keep an eye open for new technology that's coming along. Here are a few simple ways to do that:

- Follow the investment and funding announcements to see what's being used in the office of the CFO and what's attracting the most funding.
- Develop a group of peers and talk to them about what they're using, and what they're looking at using.
- Read the marketing emails you get from technology companies. Though you might feel you're getting sold to, some of those emails will feature a great product. Think about whether this product might make sense for you, and reply so you can at least get some information about it.

Keep an open mind for anything that could make you better at your job, and that can make the work easier. Always keep learning so you don't stagnate. The only way to change the paradigm is to stay on top of the latest technology and to keep trying different ways to do things.

RELATIONSHIPS

The unfortunate stereotype of an accountant is an introvert who would rather hide in a corner working on a spreadsheet that no one else will ever care about, but it does highlight what can be a big deficit in skills. Our accounting training is heavy on theory, and light on interpersonal skills. Relationships is a big bucket of skills, and encompasses the distinct areas of leadership, communication, empathy, and generosity, as well as developing relationships with other peers.

Leadership Skills

As Mike discussed at length in his previous book, *Controller's Code,* a big shift that accountants need to make as they move up the ranks and into the controller's seat is stepping into a leadership role. Leadership isn't just about making sure the people below you get their work done. Leadership is about creating an environment where people are empowered and excited to do their best work. Great leaders increase the likelihood that everyone is doing all they can to contribute to the grand vision of the organization.

If you're reading this book, you've most likely noticed that the most effective leaders in an organization aren't necessarily the ones with the elevated job titles but are generally the ones who people listen to and follow. As leadership guru John Maxwell said, "Leadership is influence. It is the ability to obtain followers." This means that even if you're not (yet) the controller or even the accounting manager, you can still be an effective leader, especially if you demonstrate the Ops mindset of wanting to make things better across the organization.

The Ops approach means you will need to have followers across the organization who are willing to change the way they do their work so that, ultimately, their lives will be better. A key skill for leading these followers across the organization is what Hugh O'Neill defines as people management: "managing people who are at your level, above your level, below your level. It's upward management, downward management, and horizontal management." Hugh says you do this by developing an understanding of the people in your organization and how they need to be managed so you can get the best out of them. You become someone who others look up to.

Our role as accountants gives us a bit of a head start at being someone people look up to in an organization, according to Shivang. "You have to understand the impact that an accountant makes when you put out fires, and you clean problems up for people."

As an accountant, you possess a specific type of knowledge that others don't. When you use your accounting superpowers for good, Shivang says you'll be rewarded with gratitude, "not just personally, but also professionally from your peers," Shivang says. But this specialized knowledge of GAAP also can be used as a weapon from the Office of No, so Shivang encourages us to use that knowledge "to be more of a consultant, and not as the rules police, but as a tool to push our organizations forward."

Leading a team is a bit different in the remote world. You lose out on those impromptu hallway and breakroom chats that let you demonstrate in person that you care about your coworkers, that you have their back. It takes more effort in today's remote world. Shivang calls it "management investment." It's more about managing the culture than managing the person. He does this at two levels: the team level and the individual level.

At the team level, Shivang keeps the culture of his remote team tightly knit with virtual events like cooking, wine tasting, or bingo. A fun one- or two-hour activity that includes some icebreakers can help people connect with their team members.

At the individual level, Shivang has regular one-on-ones by video with those he's managing. Midway through his video chats or near the end, he asks some simple, open-ended questions: "How are you doing? Is there anything going on? Is there anything I can help with? Is there anything you want to bounce off of me?" He frames it as two people just chatting with no judgment. Whether the answer is "my mom's dealing with this, or here's what I'm struggling with at work, or my pet has this going on," Shivang welcomes all three of those scenarios because it builds a better connection between him and his team members. Almost every time he asks those simple questions, he sees the other person's face relax, and open up, which is exactly what he's looking for.

Those connections build mutual trust. "The leader needs to absolutely trust their team," he says. "If you trust your team, you don't need to micromanage them." Not only do you not need to micromanage your team, but when team members see you taking time as their leader to build that connection, he finds that their "productivity level as an employee is gonna go through the roof." Shivang is surprised that more leaders don't take advantage of this tactic to get people to do their best work. Of course, some are just slammed with work. But, as he says, "the simple question of 'How are you doing?' can go a long way."

As we touched on earlier in this chapter, getting to know the VPs in your organization is critical. It seems so simple, but if people like you more personally, you'll get more stuff done at work. At the basic level, that means taking the VP of product out for lunch, or having drinks or coffee or something. Those simple gestures add up to an easier time on your next initiative.

Another aspect of leadership that accountants may struggle with is learning to be more assertive. Jaysen Dyal, FloQast Product Marketing Manager, says the "general personality trait that fits an accountant is that they tend to be too quiet." In contrast to the sales reps and marketing people and engineers who know how to push what they want, accountants tend to be happy to leave their concerns on the back burner. "Accountants have to find a way to throw their hat into the ring to get some improvements," Jaysen says. Assertiveness is definitely a trait accountants need to work on to take on an operational role. You have to be willing to push people and lead people throughout the organization to adopt and adhere to the changes you want, so that everything gets better for everyone.

Clear Communication Skills

A crucial aspect of leadership is becoming a better communicator. Most people don't go into accounting because they envision themselves as being future leaders or being great at communicating. And those aren't the characteristics that people associate with accountants. But both of these are what organizations need from accountants, and both are the skills that most accountants need to start developing immediately.

As we discussed at length in Chapter 7, within organizations, what we see as the two biggest things that hold companies back are the issues of perception and communication. Clear communication can help bridge that gap, both in asking enough questions that you understand the other person's perspective, and in helping the other person understand what parameters you're operating under.

Our job as controllers is actually communication. We're communicating economic events through numbers. The reporting isn't just for the sake of reporting, but the goal of reporting should be to communicate economic activity so that leadership can make good decisions. While our education and training has focused on financial statements — a very unique form of communication — we have to remember that conveying the information to the broader organization has always been part of our responsibility. And, as mentioned in Chapter 7, not everyone understands the language of accounting. We need to also become better at telling the story around the financials, filling in the context of what was happening in the organization, the industry and the broader economy, and connecting that with the broader goals of the organization.

The ability to clearly communicate complex accounting issues can have a domino effect. Shivang Patel previously worked with a controller who had a sound operational sense of accounting and who could also explain complex topics in "a way that was common sense." After his controller "broke down sales tax in a very conversational way," Shivang was able to leverage that understanding to immediately fix a tax error that someone else was having. "In turn, I was able to improve that individual's knowledge where she was able to help her peers in the future with similar issues," he recalls.

Communication skills are crucial for building connections across the company, according to Hugh O'Neill. "You can be the best accountant in the world, but if nobody wants to talk to you, you're pretty useless. That's your job." You need the balance of technical skills, knowing what to do, and making it accurate alongside talking to people, getting the information, piecing it all together, and finding the value because "that's ultimately what will lead to success," says Hugh.

New accountants are often surprised at the amount of writing that accountants do. However, you're not writing *War and Peace*. It's more like distilling that entire novel into a few pages or even a paragraph or two. You have to learn to be concise. As Jaysen Dyal says, "your footnote can be 10 pages, but you have to be able to get it down to a paragraph and tell a whole story in a paragraph." The writing we do can range from a very brief explanation of a variance to bullet points on a slide deck to memos to reports (or even books like this one). Whatever it is, it needs to be clear and unambiguous.

Besides writing, you also need good presentation skills. Adam Schall did a great job while he was at FloQast of putting materials together and walking people through his information in a way that was easy to understand. Besides putting together presentations, you also need to be able to talk to people in ways that help you get them to cooperate with the changes you'll be asking them to make. As you push through initiatives and take on a bigger leadership role at your company, you will need to be comfortable presenting in front of a group of people.

Accountants don't tend to be known for their skill with words, so if this is you, we have a couple ideas. A book that Mike especially recommends is *Thank You for Arguing*, by Jay Heinrichs. Arguing has a very negative connotation, but as

Heinrichs writes, "The basic difference between an argument and a fight: an argument, done skillfully, gets people to do what you want. You fight to win; you argue to achieve agreement."

When Mike and FloQast co-founder Cullen Sandstrom both read that book, their whole working relationship changed. It taught Mike how to get his point across and how to persuade people to do what he wanted them to do, without being a bully. Mike describes this as "a book on rhetoric that has really helped me step back from any discussion that was heading into confrontational waters, and guide it where I needed it to go. I use these ideas when I talk to investors, to the board, to the executive team, and to the whole team."

Another idea for improving speaking skills is to consider joining Toastmasters. As Mike wrote in his previous book, *Controller's Code: The Secret Formula For a Successful Career in Finance,*

> *When I first founded FloQast, I was pretty terrible at public speaking. Like most people, and like most accountants in particular, I didn't have much practice at it. It's not something they teach along with revenue recognition.*
>
> *But I knew that public speaking was something I needed to improve at. So I joined Toastmasters and went to meetings for a couple months. At Toastmasters, I found a super supportive environment. Everyone there was just trying to get better at public speaking. We would have practice sessions, and critique each other. It was a very trusting environment. What I loved most was that I learned the specific areas I needed to work on.*
>
> *It was really helpful. It gave me confidence that I'm actually not as bad at public speaking as I thought I was.*

The communication part can be really difficult, but it's

crucial for making change happen. Anytime you're making changes, you need to find ways to get people to make those changes and to buy in on your idea.

Communication is about learning to sell people on your point of view, and to convince them that on the other side of this big change, there's a light. Everybody can have a better life. You need to sell people on why it's in their best interest to follow the new process. Some team members will adhere to the new process just because you told them to. But others will need a reason that makes sense to them, which brings us to the next crucial skill.

Empathy

Moving into Ops means constantly shifting to another's perspective. If you're just stuck in your own world, you might not consider how the ways that you pass off work might affect the way another person does their job. By making it easier for accounting, you may be making it harder for someone else. This is what the operational accountant needs most of all to address and to understand.

Jonathan Hardy, Director of FP&A at LeadVenture, says an important skill he's learned with the Ops approach is the ability to see things from different perspectives, particularly when there are disagreements about the ways that information is transferred between parties. "You have to take a more understanding approach to try to figure out what angle the other person is coming from. Why do they need it the way they need it? Why do I need it the way I need it? Is there a compromise?" Jonathan says.

Besides helping him to consider the perspectives of others, the Ops approach has forced Jonathan "to have difficult conversations with people," a skill he can apply both at work and outside of work. The Ops approach has helped him learn to talk disagreements out, "to get to some reasonable agreement, or just agree that you disagree" — a useful skill in today's world and in furthering one's career. "You can't just go in and say no or plant a stake in the ground. It won't get you very far in an organization, and people won't like working with you," he adds.

Most people in an organization are focused primarily on what's in it for them and on getting their job done. So being able to talk to people all across the organization, hearing what their jobs are, understanding what their day-to-day concerns are, and then taking that into account with what you're doing in your job will make everyone's life better. According to Hugh O'Neill, "you won't know all the intricacies about what's going on, but you can at least check in and ask the right questions to get the right information out of them." Hugh also believes that developing an inquisitive nature and to always be learning is key to doing good work in operations, even if it goes against your nature as an accountant. "It's a lot of learning, and you're out of your comfort zone. You're taking on a different role, and it's kind of uncomfortable."

Controllers see the world through the lens of accounting, which can make it hard for us to understand the priorities of others, and for others to understand our priorities. Though we're honestly just trying to get our work done, others across the company — and even sometimes within accounting — don't really understand what we need or what we're trying to do. Our focus is on data and systems and reporting, which can be foreign to people in other parts of the organization. Data and reporting and systems are all we see from our version of Plato's cave while other parts of the organization have their own cave shaping their perceptions of what's important. So they get frustrated and we get frustrated. We're trying to effect change from our lens of accounting.

Stefan compares it to the priorities that different kinds of doctors have. "A dermatologist will say the number one thing you need to do is wear sunscreen because they see melanoma all the time. But a heart doctor will say that the number one thing you need to do is not eat salt or high-fat foods because all they see is heart disease. But as an individual, those are two very different things, and very different risks." We need to acknowledge that the accounting lens is not very well understood by the broader organization, and that likewise, we may not really understand the marketing lens or the product lens. Taking on operations means we need to take responsibility for those differing lenses and do our best to step into the shoes of others.

Giving is Better Than Receiving

Besides seeing the work from others' perspectives and learning to communicate in terms that make sense to them, adopting an attitude of generosity will help in strengthening relationships. Shivang relates a valuable lesson that our CRO, Ken Sims, taught him. "In sales, you don't ask, you give. And when you as a salesperson start to learn that giving is better than asking, you'll receive tenfold in return." While this lesson was specifically about sales, this is just as applicable to Ops. Shivang continues:

> *As accountants, we get so busy with our day-to-day, but if you take a few minutes and fix a report, fix a system issue, or create a new field, when you go above and beyond to do that for somebody else in your company, the reward that you'll be given will be worth it.*

By putting in a little more effort on the front end, and

working a little longer, despite a never-ending to-do list, we can often avoid issues on the back end.

Build Relationships With Other Controllers

Not many people actually do this, but the ones who have a community group or peer network they can reach out to will benefit in a major way. It's not always high-level questions that get discussed. Mike asked a group of controllers what they were discussing in their recent meetings and they said that right now, the big topic was "What should an org chart look like?" This sounds like basic stuff, but in contrast to other parts of an organization that might be able to just paste in an org chart they get from a consulting firm, teams in finance and accounting tend to be structured differently. It's almost like the org chart is structured based on the strengths and weaknesses of whomever was in the building at the time, which isn't necessarily the perfect end state. So, this peer network was learning from each other the variety of structures in place among them. It's not really a topic that a controller would want to discuss with their CFO, but in a peer network, they could explore in depth.

Even just reaching out to another controller can be helpful. When Stefan was controller at Kodiak Cakes, he would regularly call up another controller in Park City as a sounding board. "Sometimes I would just vent, and he would work on a report in the background. At the end, I would thank him, and he'd say, 'I didn't tell you anything, you solved your own problem.' It was always a two-way street with us. I'd do the same thing for him." Sometimes you just need someone to talk to without judgment and to give you the affirmation, and then you can go execute.

Sometimes the controllers you meet are at a slightly different point in their careers than you. Those ahead of you can be mentors, which can help you become a better controller. This was the case for Stefan when he met a controller who was a few years ahead of him at a slightly larger company. "It gave me the option to bounce ideas off someone I trusted, to hear his perspective. It was almost foreshadowing because I would hear him complain about stuff, and then I'd experience it six months or a year later." That mentorship was critical for Stefan's success as a controller.

EXECUTION

Execution is how the work gets done, how the changes are made, and how things get better. It's how a company acts like an army, rather than as random individuals, all contributing on their own to something they don't fully understand. The Ops approach gets everyone working together, with better intention and efficiency. You may still be doing the same thing, but you're doing it without the siloed approach getting in the way of trying to execute.

Execution itself can be slotted into three buckets: collaboration, project management, and change management.

Collaboration

Collaboration is an essential part of both relationships and execution. It's required today for effective leadership, which isn't the old-school "I'm the boss, so do it my way" approach, but is more about partnering with others in your organization.

The cool part about developing relationships across your organization is that it makes collaboration way easier, and way more effective. If you came up through audit, you've most likely already had experience working in a collaborative setting. Each team member has their tasks, and if it's a true team effort, you help each other so you can get the audit out the door, on deadline, and move on to the next one. And if you've made the effort as a controller to develop relationships across functions, then you'll have a much easier time getting people to at least listen to your ideas.

But how do you foster collaboration if your organization is pretty siloed to begin with? Here's the approach we use at FloQast, which we encourage you to try out, as a way to begin building connections between functions.

When we have a cross-functional initiative, we put together a group of people across those functions who will be responsible for that initiative, and we assign a point person to own it. Then every Monday at our C-level meeting, the people assigned to all of the initiatives present at that meeting. So in those meetings, we have people from different groups, presenting to all of their bosses and all of the other bosses at the same time. By bringing everyone together, we can get everything out on the table. You can keep track of everything, and keep the wheels in motion.

Yes, it's weird for a controller to do this. But if you're trying to drive an initiative, you should be calling a meeting and owning that meeting, and including everyone involved in that project. Those meetings need to happen on a regular basis, whether it's weekly, monthly, quarterly, or whatever makes sense for your organization. The key part is presenting as a group to all of your bosses to ensure that you are being transparent about what's going on, and that everyone's being held accountable for getting that work done.

The goal in pushing collaboration is to be the one people turn to when they want advice. So when the sales team has a new idea for running contracts that they think will drive a lot of sales, they'll come to you and ask what you think. That's always better than finding out later, painfully, when they just toss a bag over the fence and crush you. But when sales lets you know ahead of time, you can get ahead of the additional flow. That communication piece ahead of time is so powerful. It lets you remove the clog from the drain before anything gets backed up.

True collaboration doesn't mean that the answer you started with is necessarily the final or best answer, but is more like a baseline of what you're trying to achieve with this change. It starts with listening to all sides and moving the pieces to see if you can build something better. Sometimes, when everyone gets everything out into the open, a new solution will emerge, one that neither side would have thought of on their own. But you can only reach that new solution when you go into the conversation with an open mind, not necessarily tied to your opinion, but seeking the best solution for everyone.

It helps if you go into these conversations with curiosity. You're trying to find the right answer. Maybe your idea is the best, or maybe you don't have all the data. The goal is to leave the meeting with a greater understanding, and a commitment to work together.

You're not dictating to them what they have to do, which you most likely can't anyways since you're not really their boss, but this process is for building trust. You need to come with an attitude of wanting to help — not control. After you've done this a few times with the same people, it gets easier because they understand the process and they understand what you need from them.

You know you've been successful at building a trusting relationship when they start coming to you for help with their pain points. Maybe it means you do something different on the accounting side that makes it easier for them, or maybe you have ideas for how they can do things differently. But the first step is creating the relationship. Then you keep the trust strong by following through on what you say you'll do.

Change Management

Dealing with change management is a huge crux of Ops and a core part of leadership. Stefan emphasizes that you can't just apply change management tactics, but you need to create change culture within your organization. To have true operational excellence, your team must embrace change. Not change for the sake of change, but change to make things better. When you present change as a means to improvement, it's not seen as a negative, or as something you need to worry about, but a way to remain on the forefront.

It's part of human nature to resist change. Habits and routines that we can follow on autopilot reduce the cognitive load. People who have been burned by change in the past may be especially resistant to new ways of doing their work. But the world of business is changing rapidly, and the pace of change we're seeing now is the slowest we will see in our lifetime. So creating change culture is imperative if you want to be around for the next 10 years, or maybe even just the next five years, because we have no idea what's around the corner.

Achieving operational excellence doesn't mean you go through a tremendous change once and you're done. It's an iterative process, a feedback loop that we explore in Chapter 10.

Change culture means constantly looking for ways to improve, and accepting feedback across the organization. It's not just staff in accounting and it can't be just one team or one set of individuals. You have to want and invite feedback from everyone, not just the controller and CFO, but all through finance, operations, sales, and every part of the organization.

Clear communication about change is essential. That clear communication needs to include both explanations of the new processes and the reasons for making the change. You can put together slide decks and write out the new processes and have your team create demo videos, but it's the human element of getting people to adhere to the changes that makes or breaks an initiative.

You have to bring people on board with the vision of what it is you're trying to change within the organization, or nothing will change. Getting people on board requires that you sell people on the reasons for making a change. You have to pitch the benefits or other reasons for making the change. You have to exercise empathy and try to see the change from their point of view. Most initiatives will fall into one of three levels in a hierarchy of change management. They are:

What's in it for me?

The easiest kinds of changes to make will have a tangible benefit to the person adopting the new process. An example is implementing an expense reimbursement piece of software. In the old days, sales could just drop a receipt on the desk of someone in accounting, and they would get reimbursed eventually. It's easy for the sales rep, but it might take a while and it might get lost in someone's inbox.

Then you implement something like Expensify, and the first reaction is pushback against the new process. But when you point out that all that someone needs to do is snap a picture of a receipt, upload it, and the reimbursement shows up on the next paycheck, the speed of reimbursement can be very appealing. This is especially true for sales reps racking up thousands in credit card charges, and who might be constantly on the road. It's also easier for accounting when everyone is actually using an expense reimbursement app instead of compiling manual expense reports. So there's a readily apparent benefit to the whole transaction chain for implementing this new process. Everyone from the sales rep to the accountant booking the entry and processing the reimbursement has an easier time, which makes it an easy change to pitch.

What's in it for the company?

If it's not purely beneficial to the person in their particular role, the next level in the hierarchy is explaining why it's best for the company overall. We're making this change because we're scaling, or because we're making these changes as an organization, or whatever is the reason for this new initiative. You can — and should — acknowledge any annoyance it will bring for an individual, but emphasizing the benefits for the company as a whole can help people get on board with the change.

This is the new process, period.

The third and final level is just cracking the whip and telling managers to force everyone to follow this new process, whether they like it or not. This is obviously not ideal, and you want to try for earlier in this hierarchy. It's more positive if people have a meaningful reason for the change. But unfortunately, a lot of accountants cut straight to this level and tell people, "That's the rule. You have to do it this way." We accountants tend to be linear, follow-the-rules, check-all-the-boxes in our approach to process changes. That tendency likely comes from audit, where if you don't follow the rules, you fail the audit. We former auditors bring that mentality over to business. But when you're running a business, you're not so worried about strict compliance. There's a gray area between the absolute rules, and there are often good reasons to work in that gray area.

Often, you can get to that first or second level by treating change discussions as a teaching moment. Stefan likens it to being in a study group in college. Unlike being a tutor or a TA, where you're giving information, in a study group it's much more conversational and your mentality is to allow yourself to learn from the other party. It's a reciprocal and collaborative process, which is incredibly important when you're working cross functionally. It goes back to perspective. You don't know everything on their end. Even though your primary focus may be on giving the other person information, you're also trying to get information and their perspective. You are trying to get to a higher level of efficiency and effectiveness together.

Both here at FloQast and at Cornerstone OnDemand, Adam Schall has overseen plenty of initiatives, and warns that change is never easy. "You can have the best change management plan possible," he says. "There's always going to be issues coming up, and there's always going to be some level of pain as far as the person being impacted." The goal for those running the projects is to minimize that as much as possible.

Proactive communication can help to manage expectations and to prepare people for future changes. Adam is a fan of drip campaigns to alert people to upcoming changes without flooding them with too much information all at once. He likes to start about three months out with an update and feeding them bits of information for the first two months using the company's preferred communication channel. Pick up the pace during the month leading up to the change with more reminders, then when you go live, "you can't have too much communication," he said. Ahead of big launches, his team spent time creating guides and putting together how-to-videos and micro-learning videos. After launch, he would set up what he called office hours support, where people can get questions answered and live hands-on assistance. Dedicated Slack channels or email distribution lists also are helpful for the people who ignore all the usual notifications. For big changes, he recommended boot camps, where everyone is in the same room for an interactive and intensive workshop.

Soliciting feedback can lead to surprising insights, as Stefan has discovered many times. Someone will ask a question because they really don't know, but "that question challenged everything I brought to the table. It's really funny how so many great ideas actually come from someone else's ignorance." Those questions from people who superficially perhaps had no right asking a question that challenged the foundation can lead you to explore a new thought process. You can often come out in a better place, or at least avoid some pitfalls.

Change management also applies when the change comes from outside of accounting. Adam Schall observed that the accounting team is often left behind when new projects get launched elsewhere in the company, which too often results in added work and lost efficiency. To avoid that, he recommended that controllers take a proactive stance and lean into the business. You can't wait for things to come to you. "You've got to stay very well connected to the pulse of the business and to the key initiatives that are going on to make sure that your team is part of the project, even if it's an informal role, as opposed to an active contributor type role," he said.

A huge challenge with many new initiatives is that your people still have their day jobs. We've all seen project launches fail because people have been asked to manage a strategic initiative on top of their day jobs. That's why Adam had a dedicated team within his operations team that managed projects as their day jobs at FloQast. We'll talk more about his three pillars approach to building an Ops team in the next chapter.

WHY ORGANIZATIONS NEED CONTROLLERS WITH THESE SKILLS

Savvy C-suite leaders want those accountants and controllers who have developed the operational mindset and skills to have a seat at the table when they need strategic advice. Controllers have a deep understanding of how a business decision will ultimately be reflected in those all-important documents: the financial statements. And, perhaps more importantly, how the numbers in the financial statements connect with what the company is trying to do and how what the company is doing connects to its North Star. The companies that are aligned fully along that axis are the ones that will make a better world.

How to make that move into a more operational approach isn't something most of us learn in classes, and we don't always have a mentor who can help us make the shift. With that in mind, our next chapter offers tactics you need for making this crucial change.

9 / HOW DO YOU MOVE INTO AN OPERATIONAL ROLE?

A gem cannot be polished without friction, nor a man perfected without trials."
—Seneca

Reading books like this one won't be all you need to do to move into a more operational role. Sometimes it happens organically, when the board tells the CFO that instead of hiring a COO, they want the CFO to be responsible for operations. However, the C-suite isn't meant to execute. They are meant to strategize. It's the role of the VP level, which as we mentioned, includes the controller, to execute on the executives' strategy. So the CFO, besides already having way too much going on, will by nature assign operations to the person who is in the position to translate strategy into tactical execution. And that person is the controller. The reasoning is that the controller knows the organization well and is good at policy, processes, and documentation. So because of their inherent skill set (and maybe adding on the skills we covered in last chapter), they're good at it. That's the most common way it happens. If there's no COO, there's a good chance that operations will land on your plate. But not every organization works that way. If you're more stuck in the bean counter role, then this chapter has ideas to help you move into a more strategic role.

MASTER THE OPS OF THE OFFICE OF CFO FIRST

Before you can go out and solve problems across your organization, you need to first have your tradecraft mastered. Don't try to solve something in operations if your order to cash isn't working internally and you don't have a vision of how you want it to work. You need to shore up your own house before you try to fix other problems. Otherwise, it's like trying to boil the ocean, which is just not possible.

Or worse: you just gum up the works if your attempt to fix a problem elsewhere runs into your own process that isn't working. That can create two separate issues. One, you risk losing authority and credibility when they see you're struggling with your own internal processes. And two, you stall the process because you can't optimize two interacting processes at once. You'll have far more credibility if you can demonstrate that through process improvements in accounting, you're able to close the books two or three days faster.

However excited you may be to expand your knowledge base beyond accounting, Hugh O'Neill says "you can't let the other stuff you want to learn come in the way of the basics." You may have a great mind for operations, he continues, but if "the accounts are a mess, and the debt isn't collected, it's no good for nobody." Getting the basics right adds to your credibility, and as people see you doing a great job, they'll be more willing to work with you. Having a strong foundation in the fundamentals makes it easier for people both inside and outside of accounting to trust you.

What's interesting about the CFO processes is that many of them are siloed to accounting and finance, but a lot of them are cross functional. Things like financial reporting and SEC reporting tend to be pretty much contained under finance. But even things like payroll and commission statement preparation require interacting with other parts of the organization. With payroll, you're collaborating with HR, and with commissions, you'll be interacting heavily with sales. Budgeting and forecasting will have you working with every department in the organization. But before you head out and start telling people how to do their jobs, you've got to have all the processes contained under the office of the CFO nailed down.

Keep in mind you're not outputting more work. The job of the controller is to produce financial statements and metrics. You give that information to the executives so they can make decisions based on those financials. You'll keep doing that. That's the job of the accountant. **What** you do will stay the same. But **how** it gets done will change.

You'll be working behind the scenes to make sure that the way that information gets to the executives is being done as efficiently as possible. And your deep involvement with Ops means that you are also creating a deeper and broader perception of what's happening to give rise to the numbers. Keep in mind that reporting isn't done just for the sake of reporting; the reason for reporting is communication. If accounting is the language of business, then the purpose of reporting is to tell a story. That deeper perception allows for better context and a richer story. If you want to be a good controller, and especially a good CFO, you need to understand the story behind the numbers, and you need to be able to craft the story behind the numbers.

In our experience, the best way to access that deeper perception you need for a richer story is to use one workflow tool for all of your reporting, whether that's FloQast (our obvious first choice) or something else. But when you have increased visibility, you gain understanding of how everyone collaborates, and you'll see where the bottlenecks really are, and what the downstream impacts of those bottlenecks are. You can see which processes you should work on first, and which you can maybe wait on.

EXPAND YOUR KNOWLEDGE BASE THROUGH DIRECT EXPERIENCE

Even before you're in the controller's seat and as you're moving up the ranks, Hugh O'Neill recommends spending time with the people who work in the different areas. If you want to understand how revenue works, go talk to the salesperson. "Ask them to help you understand the process. Ask them, 'What's going on? What are the trends? How can I help?'" Hugh says. As you work with different people in different functions, and if you get on with them, they'll teach you different bits around the business, and that will ultimately help you. Hugh liked working in small businesses "because you could do everything. There was an element that it was all under your control. You had to learn to do lots of different things."

Understanding the sales process and understanding the product is fundamental to the Ops approach, according to Jerry Raphael, CFO of Hypori. "I would encourage CPAs and accountants to get in touch with the product, understand who the customer is, and why they are buying the product," said

Jerry. "Put yourself in the shoes of the other company that's buying the product and see how this product helps them move forward." Jerry even took the step of going through his company's sales training to become certified to sell the product. That training helped him understand why contracts were written the way they were, how the sales team was structured and what motivated them, as well as clarifying the accounting for those sales contracts.

Besides understanding the accounting side, a deeper knowledge of the sales process and the product will help you in your career progression, Jerry says, especially if you aspire to be CFO or CEO, because you're going to interact with the board, the investors, and other stakeholders. "The number one topic on everyone's mind is sales," Jerry says. "Where are we with sales? How are we doing, and how can we move things forward faster? What are the leading indicators that tell us we're going in the right direction?" On the product side, you'll want to learn as much as you can about the product, including how it's built and distributed, and the relationships with other partners involved in any stage — from production, to delivery, to customer experience.

The CEO and board members wake up every day thinking about these operational elements, and if you want to have meaningful conversations with the leaders of your company, Jerry says these are the topics that will come up. "It's never going to be, 'Did you have a hard time making this accrual? Or was it easy to book that journal entry?'" Jerry says.

Chris Sluty agrees that moving up to the controllership level means you need to develop an understanding of how the company operates. As a staff accountant, "you might only be looking at a segment of the balance sheet," but as you move up, you gain a better understanding of how the business operates by "asking those questions, and stepping away from just your area and just trying to get the work done that period."

Establishing relationships with people across the company helps you learn how to talk to different people and see how they interact. It can also be helpful when you step into a broader role. As Hugh O'Neill says, "I could bounce ideas and problems off people who weren't necessarily on my team. The more people you have exposure to, the more you learn. You can broaden out, you can talk to different people, you can get different ideas and different solutions."

Another recommendation from Hugh is to offer to take things off the controller's plate. "Quite often, controllers can be quite rushed, and they don't want to do everything," he says. So they can be quite open to dividing and conquering the work, and getting an extra set of eyes on the work. But you have to also be sure that you're still getting the fundamentals of your position done. You can't let the basics of your day job slip. "If you can take some more of this operational work off them," Hugh adds, "I think most controllers will be happy to help you learn and develop." On the other had, if your controller isn't open to assigning new responsibilities to you, Hugh says, "There's a question to be asked about whether they're the right person to be working for."

When the controller has more time to think because you're taking things off their plate and you're turning in accurate work, Hugh says that allows the controller to ask deeper questions, which is ultimately better for the business. For example, if there's a payment run and the numbers don't match, the controller could spend all their time checking reams of paper and individual invoices to find the mistake, "as opposed to sitting back and thinking 'should I be paying this invoice, or should I not be paying this invoice?' You can only think about what you're thinking about."

If your organization is using a flux analysis tool, Chris Sluty recommends getting a deeper understanding of how the business works by looking at the "period-over-period change and explaining why things change, and taking a higher-level analytical approach." This helps you see "how the pieces fit together, and not just looking at your subsection." Even better is if you have the opportunity to go through a flux analysis with the CFO and "making sure you are asking those secondary questions for your better understanding of how the business functions," Chris says. Developing that baseline will go a long way in helping you work with people across different parts of the business. "If you only know the revenue process, well, that's going to give you a leg up when you're talking to the sales folks," Chris says. However, that limited understanding won't get you too far if you're working on a different project and "you don't have that visibility" into the processes in that area. Gaining that visibility and deep understanding of the business and the business model is one of the most important things you can work on if you want to keep moving up in your career, says Chris.

CONSIDER SPENDING TIME IN INTERNAL AUDIT.

If you're just starting out in industry, you might want to spend some time in internal audit, as Dante Giannini described to us on our "Blood, Sweat & Balance Sheets" podcast. "I didn't appreciate the impact it was going to have on my career later on," he said. "I joined as an associate level internal auditor and realized that I could make some real big contributions." By taking on an engagement that the company had partially outsourced, Dante realized that the way most companies were looking at SOX was all wrong. "They weren't looking at SOX as an augmentation of their controls, but they were looking at it as a way to justify how they were doing things already." By looking for ways to make meaningful checkpoints and controls, he developed a mindset that helped him later on as he took on an operational role. "Later on in my career, I realized how transformational that was for me. Being able to step back and eliminate things that didn't make sense to make sure that the controls were in the right place, without having to horribly destroy our processes was fantastic."

Another impactful experience that came out of Dante's time in internal audit was learning how to present to the board and to the audit committee about how they were still addressing risk, even as they eliminated controls that weren't effective.

His time in internal audit helped him to "not just think about the fundamental accounting, but to also think about how the different processes were working. How are all the pieces from outside accounting flowing into accounting? Are those other pieces including the right information?" That entire way of thinking prepared him for an operational role later.

This isn't a new and radical idea. For 110 years, starting in 1910, GE had an intensely challenging leadership training program called the Corporate Audit Staff Program (CAS), which sent young hires through an intensive, five-year, multi-division, and multi-country program with real-world training in internal audit, technology and operations, as an article in Business Insider describes.[1] Internally, this was known as the Green Beret program, and it was so challenging that only about 2% of participants actually completed it and landed an executive position at the end. At the time the Business Insider article was written (2015), 80% of GE's top CFOs were CAS members. However, in 2020, GE disbanded this program and split the program into separate internal leadership training programs in the different business units and a separate path for internal audit.[2]

PITCH YOURSELF AS A PROBLEM SOLVER

Now if you're already in the controller's seat, but you're operating in a very siloed company, and either not encouraged or actively discouraged from talking to other departments to give recommendations on how to make things better, then you'll have to take a proactive stance. Mike suggests going to the CFO and having a conversation about the increasingly operational role that accountants are taking on.

Explain that you want a more operational role as part of your career trajectory, and that you'd like to do that in your current company. Ask for the opportunity to step into a more operational role. Be sure to offer up a few ideas about how you can be more operational. Be prepared to discuss the first three things you'd like to do as part of your position, based on your interactions across the company, and the processes you think can be made more efficient. You have to be proactive with your career development, or you will remain stuck in a boring role.

If the CFO is willing to listen, Mike says the next thing you'll need is a solid plan for solving the biggest bottleneck. The CFO may not know that the problems you want to solve even exist, so you may need to paint a picture of the situation, with numbers to back up your story if possible. The kinds of process issues that you might want to work on probably aren't even on their radar, so you may need to pitch it in terms that they care about, like cutting days off the close, or not needing additional headcount to scale.

You'll make the biggest impression if you go in with a solid solution and a plan to make it happen. You'll need a budget to purchase technology if that's part of the solution, and, if it's a big enough change, you may need the CFO's blessing to pull together a task force with representatives from all the departments involved. Lay out a timeline for making this happen, and paint a solid picture of the benefits to the company after this change is made.

The last thing you want to do is go in to the CFO with a problem and ask their advice on how to fix it. Mike, like most CEOs, hates the problem-focused approach. If you want to take on Ops, you've got to be solution-oriented. It's not your job to complain about bottlenecks. It's your job to identify and fix those bottlenecks.

Hopefully, the CFO says yes to your pitch, so you go and execute on that, and knock off that first project. And now, everyone, and especially the CFO, sees that numbers are more accurate, the work is getting done faster, and the financials are getting to the CFO sooner, or whatever the result of your first big project is. If it was a problem that the CFO wasn't even aware of, your effort is much more impactful. They see that you as controller have your ear to the ground and you know what's going on. And they'll trust you even more to make sure that everything continues to get better. Then you work on the next biggest bottleneck, chipping away at the problems one at a time.

Stefan, whose experience in the controller seat gives him a slightly different perspective, says a key to getting the CFO on board is stepping into their shoes. CFOs tend to be very finance focused, in contrast to controllers, who are accounting focused. Even the CFOs who came up through accounting frequently switch to a finance focus once they step into that role.

Finance and accounting are two very different personas, and each has a different approach to their work. Both areas take years to hone their professional abilities, but a big difference is that finance doesn't always have the technical knowledge base that accountants start from. Stefan says, "You can teach an accountant finance, but you can't teach a finance person accounting because that base technical knowledge is so difficult to come by." CFOs who came up through finance tend not to understand what accounting teams do every day, every month, and every quarter.

CFOs often struggle to grasp the details of accounting, so a controller who can translate that information into terms that they can understand can be a huge help to the CFO. This will help the CFO understand the accounting at a deeper level than most in the broader organization, but they most likely will still be missing a good chunk of the details that the controller deals with day to day.

Besides having the finance perspective versus the accounting focus, CFOs tend to be pulled in two very different directions. While they are trying to affect change in their organizations to build more resilient and efficient companies, they need to balance that push for change with the traditional tasks they're responsible for. They're still in charge of audits, tax, and other compliance matters that controllers don't think about daily.

CFOs can be very effective in pushing for improvements in Ops, simply from the authority of their position. This can put CFOs in sort of a weird pinch, where they're trying to affect change, but don't necessarily have the hands-on expertise in the areas that they're trying to change. An Ops-minded controller can support the CFO by helping to fill in the areas of understanding that a CFO may be lacking.

FOCUS ON YOUR PRIORITIES

We all want to fix everything all at once, but that's impossible. You're going to have a long list of things you can improve. You can't execute well and you can't act with intention if you're trying to do it all. Both of us have had experiences where we've tried to execute with excellence on 10 things, and they're all pulling in different directions. Ten projects in flight is just a grind.

Instead of trying to do those 10 or 100 things at once, sort them by impact, pick your top two or three priorities, and work on those. Just focusing on a few things will relieve the mental strain of all those different projects tugging at you. Psychologically, it's better to get some wins. With fewer projects, you can get something done. You score a little dopamine hit, and move to the next one with more confidence. The wins come faster, and you can chip away at the changes gradually.

Mike always uses the lame quote for continuous improvement, "Water wears away stone," because it's true. Once a month or once a quarter, look to see what your biggest bottleneck is, and start chipping away at those and get them off your plate. Then, in a year or two or three, when you pick up your head, you'll see that you have a smooth stone instead of a jagged boulder, and your department is going to be way better before you even know it. Just take it one step at a time.

DO THE WORK

Certainly, you can have a conversation with your boss around the importance of operations, but Mike's favorite way to get a job is to just force your way into that role and start doing it. It takes a certain amount of panache to do that, but Mike is a big believer in this idea.

Say you realize that the sales order process is a mess and you need to get it sorted out to make your life easier. You have to go over to sales, and start interacting with that team, which is a whole new dynamic. You have to go in knowing you're going to step on some toes, and you have to have confidence that what you will propose is going to be right for the business. If you just do the job for enough time, you are going to be more qualified than the vast majority of people.

BUILD AN OPS TEAM AROUND THREE FOUNDATIONAL SKILL SETS

If you keep working in Ops long enough, you'll need to build a team. As Jim Collins wrote in *Good to Great*, the first step is to get the right people on the bus, and the next is to get those people in the right seats on that bus. Stefan says that building and maintaining the right team are two of the biggest pain points for controllers. It's really hard "to have the right individuals, know when to let someone go, know when to hire someone, who to hire, and know what's coming down the pipeline." But without dedicated people to take ownership and project manage, you will be guaranteeing failed initiatives and crappy project deployments.

When the time comes to build an Ops team, Adam Schall recommends building it around three skill sets: Business Systems, Business Operations, and Business Intelligence. Let's look at these in order.

Business Systems oversees administration, development, and integrations of core applications like Salesforce and NetSuite. In many startups, it can become the wild west in your core applications if you don't have someone who develops a deep knowledge and discipline around how the core applications interact. Without that knowledge base, it's far too easy to ask the developers to solve problems by adding a bit of code or a new field here or there. Eventually, that uncoordinated hacking can create such a complicated web of code that any seemingly small change can break a million other things, which can make fixing it nearly impossible without spending a lot of time and money. Developing this knowledge base and skill set early on can help limit those ad-hoc approaches to fixing problems.

Business Operations serves as internal consultants for the whole company. While the functional operations like sales ops or marketing ops have the depth of knowledge in their domains, business operations has the breadth of knowledge across the company and can connect the dots between the different functions. To be effective in this role, you'll need people with project management skills who have (or can acquire) a basic understanding of the different functions across the organization. These people can serve as project managers for big initiatives, or they can jump into any part of the business to help out. They might not know the details of exactly how things work in a particular area, but they know enough to be able to coordinate the various teams that need to work together on a particular project. Having a dedicated person or group of people who can manage big strategic initiatives means you're not asking someone to oversee a big project on top of doing their day job, which gives those projects a better chance of success.

Business Intelligence makes sure that everyone is using the same single source of truth in their reporting. The first step is developing a BI platform that leadership and management can use as their one place to go to for data that may be coming from many different sources. That one tool might be pulling from different source systems, but the data is all integrated in one place and is properly governed. Once you have that platform, your business intelligence people can help others across the organization access and understand the data they need for their particular function.

The other key to building a smoothly functioning Ops team is to share your knowledge and learnings with your team to avoid creating what Shivang Patel calls "a bottleneck leader." If you don't pass that knowledge on to your team, "you've just created the ability for you to be the go-to every single time there is an issue, and asked for a lot more on your to-do list," he says. Instead, Shivang says a smarter approach is to "replicate yourself into 10 or 12 people," which limits the number of requests on your time. This also has the benefit that "you're actually perceived by your bosses in a better light" because those extra 10 or 12 extensions of yourself mean "there's less concern of inaccurate numbers or a bad strategy." Shivang says that bringing people up around you and molding them to be better than you will pay off in any role in the company, not just in accounting.

LEAN INTO FRICTION

Stefan believes that what made him effective in his first job as controller was a very sharp and demanding boss at Skullcandy, "It was constant. She was always after me. 'Do this better. Do that better,'" Stefan recalled. "And in the moment, it kind of sucks. But at the end of it, if you rise to the challenge, you come out a much stronger individual." It challenged him to always up his game, and as Stefan's boss and her boss realized he could do more, they expected more. "Skullcandy really cut my teeth and tempered me to be a controller."

Throughout this book, we've been hammering on the idea that a goal of achieving operational excellence is to reduce friction. But in any business, there will always be friction. You'll always have the five points of pressure hammering on you. The business landscape is always changing. Laws and regulations are always changing. Technology changes constantly. We need friction to grow. If your life doesn't have friction, you're probably not growing.

Fixing problems is like lowering the water level in a stream. More rocks will surface as the water level drops, and you've got to address the new problems as they arise. You can't sit there complacent and ignore the friction that's bothering you.

Friction is actually good. You don't know that something's wrong until there's friction. You won't address it until there's friction. All of life needs friction to grow. You don't grow muscles without friction, without tearing and destroying and rebuilding.

If your organization seems frictionless, there's probably something very wrong going on, and you just have no idea. Businesses that seem frictionless are stagnant. And if they remain stagnant, they die. You might be able to get by for a while before a competitor notices that your business isn't moving forward, which gives that competitor permission to take over your shared space. It doesn't matter what the industry is, or how big the company is. If there's no friction and no growth, something is wrong or will go wrong soon.

The same can be said about your career. If you're not feeling friction and pressure, you're not growing anymore. One of the reasons Stefan came over to FloQast was that he didn't feel he was growing significantly in his career as an accountant anymore. "I've mastered a lot of things, and I can still definitely improve a thousand things in accounting, but those weren't big changes anymore. They were really small, incremental changes. And I felt like I was losing my edge." So at FloQast, Stefan works in marketing, which he knew nothing about before he came over. Those new challenges are helping him maintain that edge and change the narrative. Many of the accountants and CPAs who work here at FloQast in all parts of the company feel the same way.

REMOTE HAS CHANGED OUR WORLD

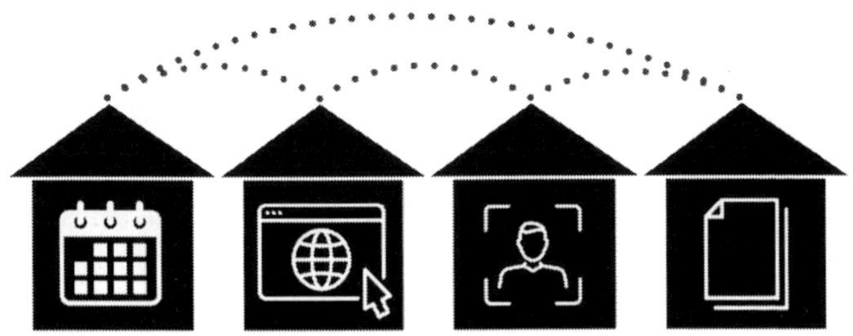

Back when we all worked on-site, we could walk down the hall and fix a problem in just a few minutes. But now, as Shivang reminds us, "The hall is a virtual hallway, and I have to be fighting cats and dogs and babies and other things that can distract me. But that's just the world we're in today. How do you operate at the same, if not faster pace, knowing that you've been dealt a completely different set of cards?" Until we went remote, we didn't realize how much time we spent keeping a pulse on things in informal ways — chatting at the watercooler, or seeing what someone was doing at their desk as we walked around the office.

Because we were forced to suddenly go remote, we learned that the technology works. Jerry Raphael, CFO of Hypori, says that "the transformation is happening in the way we do things." Because we no longer need to travel to have face-to-face conversations, Jerry observes that "We saw companies going public remotely, and that was OK. I've seen companies close funding rounds remotely. Even M&A work, where companies get bought 100% remotely." Remote work also is making it easier to find talent, so now Jerry has team members across the country, from Seattle to North Carolina. "I don't really think twice about where they are," Jerry said. "I just try to hire the best person. If you have an internet connection, and you're on the moon, and you have the right skills, I might hire you."

But even as remote work becomes more and more normalized, employers continue to be uneasy about whether their people are really working. A recent Microsoft Work Trends Study[3] found just how different perceptions between employees and employees are. While 87% of employees thought they were more productive remotely or with a mix of in-office and remote work, almost the same number of employers (85%) weren't confident that their employees are productive in a hybrid environment. The result for many employers is to add yet more surveillance methods so they can track meaningless productivity measures such as keystrokes or mouse movements. At a recent conference,[4] Microsoft CEO Satya Nadella pushed back on this trend, saying that this is the wrong data to track and can have other negative consequences: "Surveillance doesn't just lead to bad data — it undermines trust, a critical factor in organizational success, that, once lost, is incredibly difficult to regain."

Here at FloQast, we couldn't agree more. But even when you're in person, you don't really know how much someone is working. Different people work in different ways, at different speeds, and at different times. It's ludicrous to think you can get one set of metrics or one tool to track what people do. You can't put everyone in the same bucket. If you try to, you'll either get organizational conflict, or you'll get an organization that attracts and retains a singular type of individual. Stefan has seen organizations that "just cultivate the same individual over and over. They don't grow because there's no friction that forces people to change their opinions and grow." It's not good for the organization, because you end up with a bunch of group thinkers.

A challenge that Jerry Raphael sees with remote work is helping new team members learn the essential skills of accounting. "How will we train these people in the future?" The new crop of accountants and finance people won't have the benefits of human interaction and being around each other, as "they learn from working their way up through the system from the most menial tasks all the way up to the most complex tasks." While tools like Slack and Zoom and Teams do help to bridge the distance, they don't completely take the place of in-person connections.

One way to bring human interaction into organizations is to sponsor company-wide or department-wide retreats. Jerry's previous employer, Stack Overflow, had annual retreats for the entire company to get together, share ideas, and train. "It made a tremendous difference," Jerry said, when he met people he'd worked with for two years during COVID but had never met in person. After sharing a drink or dinner, his relationships with others opened up: "I'm not Jerry, the CFO. I'm the human being, and we connected on this silly thing. Maybe we both have a cat, or we both garden, or we both play guitar, whatever it might be. But it all goes back to that human interaction. It brings you closer."

Going remote also exacerbated what Stefan considers the two biggest issues in organizations: communication and perception, which we discussed in Chapter 7. Even when we were all working on site, this was an issue, and going remote made it worse. Few people are able to develop the broad and deep business view of what's happening across an organization. Those few with that ability are paid extremely well and they're usually really impactful to their organizations. Because this is such a rare trait, Stefan says it's best to just assume people don't have those skills and offer them a tech tool to use in its place.

You need a tool that's flexible enough that people aren't forced into a particular structure, and that's agile enough to change as the organization grows. Not to toot our own horn, but a tool like FloQast will give you that visibility so you can keep on top of what's going on across the organization, whether you're in the office or remote. And we give you that visibility in an objective way.

The ideas in this chapter have mainly focused on the ways you can demonstrate leadership and a mindset shift to change the trajectory of your career and your company. But because we accountants love checklists and processes, the next chapter presents the playbook we use internally at FloQast for optimizing processes.

10 / CREATING YOUR WORKFLOW PLAYBOOK

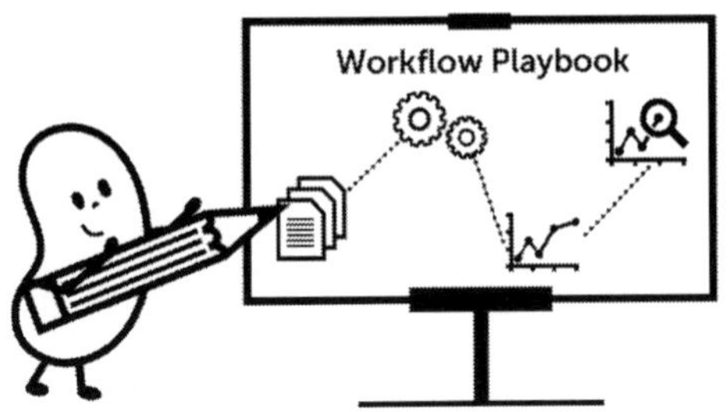

The best laid plans of mice and men often go awry.
—Robert Burns

Even when FloQast was just Mike, Cullen, and Chris, we relied on workflows to keep things running. Chris, who had never closed the books before, used the checklist workflow created by Mike in the very first iteration of FloQast to close the books his first month on the job. Completing the same tasks in the same order each month means that we can more reliably compare the results from this month to six months ago and to six months from now.

Every company has workflows for getting the work done. At the beginning, when everyone is just focused on getting the product out the door, whether that product is pancake mix or SaaS or accounting services, there are a lot of ad hoc ways of getting the work done. After a while, most people develop a routine way of doing their job — a workflow. Maybe someone showed them how to do it, maybe they figured it out on their own. With some workflows, someone might have documented it with checklists or flowcharts or something else. Other workflows may be stored inside someone's head.

But the most successful companies eventually discover that getting those workflows out of someone's head and documenting them so others can use them is a key to growth. You can't grow if someone is the bottleneck, and you can't grow if your workflows aren't efficient. You might struggle to hit deadlines if your workflows aren't efficient.

"Having a documented process really helps with visibility, but also helps with tracking towards deadlines," says Chris Sluty. It's not just the close process where there's value in creating organized processes, but anywhere in the company where there are repeatable processes. Chris continues, "Visibility, tracking the process, and documenting the process is just huge. And I think that's why people have made the leap from the close process to other operational workflows." These forward-thinking controllers are applying the same level of visibility, collaboration, and organization they've gotten by improving their close to other areas of their businesses.

Now admittedly we're biased in recommending you put your workflows in FloQast Ops, and we do think we've created the best tool out there. But whether you use FloQast or Excel or OneNote or even just a Google doc, until you create a workflow playbook that everyone has access to and actually uses, you may find your team reinventing the wheel, or — worse — coming to a screeching halt when the person who usually handles some task is unexpectedly unavailable. But if you have a workflow playbook, it's much easier for someone else to pick up the ball and run with it.

THE FLOQAST PLAYBOOK

Here at FloQast, we use the playbook in the graphic below:

You'll notice this is a circular iterative process, because you'll never reach perfection. If you're a student of Six Sigma or any other process improvement methodology, the concept of a feedback loop probably looks familiar. Feedback loops are among the most powerful ways to effect change, so this is the model we've chosen at FloQast.

STEP 1: DOCUMENT

"The checklist gets the dumb stuff out of the way, the routines your brain shouldn't have to occupy itself with."
-Atul Gawande

First, sit down with one person and ask them to walk you through exactly what he or she does. Include financial and nonfinancial players in your walk-throughs. Make sure you understand where this process fits in overall, and what the objective is. What kicks it off? What's the output and where does it go? Document all the processes, policies, and procedures, as they are currently being applied. Tag the critical data points along the way. Ask the person if there's something they need to do their job that the accounting team doesn't know about.

Walk-throughs are super important, not only from a process point of view, but also in helping you understand how the different parts of a company operate. Every industry and every company in that industry and every department within a company has its own ways of getting the work done. While there are plenty of commonalities, it's important to come in with a fresh set of eyes, as if you are a blank slate with no idea of how this person does their job or how the process is supposed to work. Ask questions about each step, so you understand the detail, while also trying to see how the process fits into the big picture.

For example, when you sit down with sales, ask them, what do you do when you negotiate a contract? What information do you need? When you're looking at your client performance, what information are you looking at? What information would be ideal?

In this process of asking about additional information, you need to watch out for scope creep. Try to talk to someone who really knows what's needed versus someone who wants a Ferrari when a Honda Accord is enough to get them there. Keep your focus on the prize, which is making things more efficient and effective for the company as a whole. Don't let perfection get in the way of the good.

Pay attention to processes that have a lot of manual work or workarounds. Find out why they have to do things the hard way. Ask about parts of the process that break, and find out why. Are there additional tools that can fix those spots? Or is the problem caused by tech that's not set up right or isn't being used correctly or at all?

Repeat this with the next step, and the next step, until you can outline a full picture of how the whole workflow works or how this part of the company operates. Use that to create a narrative and a flowchart.

Along the way, you might discover that this process captures nonfinancial data you weren't aware of. Next comes the hard part: figuring out if the data is necessary or redundant. As you tag the data that's being gathered along the way, flag the data that actually goes somewhere and is used somewhere else. Oftentimes, there's really low visibility into the data flows. Someone might have been told to collect data and enter it somewhere, but over the years, the knowledge of why it's being collected and who uses it has been forgotten.

You might need help from someone in IT to figure out whether there's a report that leverages the data, and who's pulling those reports. Sometimes this data is used for decisions you're not familiar with, so make sure that there really isn't a use for this data before you decide it's no longer needed.

Along with capturing data as it flows through the system

Adam Schall says that we also need to "make sure we're picking up the right data, and it's accurate along the way."

STEP 2: AUTOMATE

We are in the infancy of what automation, robotics and AI will ultimately do. In the words of Hugh O'Neill, "in 10 years' time, what the profession looks like, and what it's doing will be fundamentally different." Systems for the traditional tasks of payroll, AP, and cash collection haven't yet "caught up to each other to integrate, but give it a few years and somebody will figure out ways to do it and to automate it and to make that process easier," he continued.

Automation and AI may change the nature of what we do, but Jaysen Dyal explains, "I don't think we're going to just wake up one day and since accounting is automated, we won't need accountants anymore. Things will always change, whether it's new standards or just trying to understand how to record something. But to transition to a more operational role, first we've got to get the time to be able to do that." Automation gives us that time.

It seems like every month, new tech tools come on the market that promise to automate new processes and tasks, so as Adam Schall says, "a big part of Ops is identifying those areas where we can leverage systems or tools to help streamline processes to replace manual processes, or just to find tools for the people who are working through those processes to do it more efficiently and effectively."

By automating what's practical, whether it's things that break or manual processes like roll-forwards that are repeated every month and putting those processes into a workflow playbook, you improve visibility and communication.

As you automate processes, pay attention to the relationship that users have with the tech they use. According to research FloQast did in partnership with the University of Georgia Consumer Analytics program,[1] the relationship that accountants have with their technology matters as much as the tech itself. These relationships tend to fall into one of three categories:

- **Adversarial:** Technology is seen as a hindrance rather than a help.
- **Routine:** Technology is functional but doesn't add value to the accountant's work or life.
- **Synergistic:** Technology is a true partner in the accountant's work.

(0 to 100 scale, with 100 being the highest level of burnout)

Adversarial
Technology seen as a hindrance rather than a help.

Routine
Technology is functional but doesn't add value to the accountant's work or life.

Synergistic
Technology is a true partner in the accountant's work.

These relationships tend to correlate with the level of burnout reported by the accountants we surveyed. That is, those with an adversarial relationship had the highest burnout scores while those with a synergistic relationship had the lowest scores. In addition, those with a synergistic relationship were less likely to make errors that required reopening the books and reported a better work/life balance. As we'll discuss later in this chapter, the true key for a synergistic relationship is full integration so that users have not just an integrated technology system, but an **integrated technology solution** — a platform that tightly integrates all the functions you need to do your work in ways that reflect your needs and the way you think, so that the tech becomes more of a partner in your work than just a tool to do your work.

While this survey only looked at accountants, it's not hard to imagine that most people in your organization also fall into one of these three categories. An overarching goal of the Ops accountant is to move as many people as possible into the synergistic bucket.

While you're automating processes and adding tech, pay attention to how your users want to work. Choosing tech that focuses on how the user wants to work rather than strictly on functionality drives better performance overall. Pay attention to who is on the development team for a particular tool, and look for tech designed by people who have done that work, because they will innately understand how people in those parts of your company want to work. That's why at FloQast, we have accountants in every part of the company. so that our products are built by accountants for the way that accountants want to work.

As you automate and add tech, Colleen Wanty, our former Director of Product Marketing, warns that these tech projects tend to have failure rates as high as 60%. "One of the biggest risks of an automation initiative is that getting people to change how they work is extremely difficult," she explained. One of the challenges is that the end users are "disconnected from building the new process into the new software, and when the 'big rollout' happens, it is so disruptive to their workflow that they reject the new process and software," she continued.

In her experience, this happens because most software implementations involve a project team that works with users to understand their requirements, and then the software is configured to meet those requirements, followed by a training and change management phase and deployment of the software to the business users. According to Colleen, "One of the biggest challenges is that these projects are trying to make big process or 'best practice' improvements and to implement new technology at the same time. This can be extremely disruptive to users who are just trying to get their job done."

Because the business user was disconnected from building the new process into the software, the deployment is so disruptive to their workflow, they reject both the new process and the software. "And hence, the rise of software as shelfware – purchased software that is either not used at all, or is used so little because the users have returned to their original tools of spreadsheets, emails and meetings to get their job done," Colleen continued. Even with the SaaS model, these projects continue to fail because they are still plagued with the old process of deploying software. "Just like on-premise software, new SaaS solutions can be a heavy lift to deploy," Colleen said. "SaaS in the title does not equal intuitive."

To reduce the risk of failure, Colleen offers this advice:

> *Approach transformation projects with the understanding that making both a technology change with a new software combined with a big business process reengineering project is a recipe for failure. It is a far better choice to choose a more iterative 'crawl' before you 'run' approach.*
>
> *First, look for SaaS solutions that for the most part can be deployed by the business user instead of having consultants or IT teams configure the solution.*
>
> *During the evaluation phase, it is critical to weigh the intuitiveness of the solution against other solutions with the goal of having the users be responsible for deploying as much*

as possible. If users are configuring the software, buy-in starts from the moment the software is installed, rather than later during the training phase.

Second, look for a solution that allows teams to implement their current processes, but gain things like visibility, easier collaboration, and centralized storage, which on their own can improve a process.

Lastly, always consider deploying the solution with a smaller subset of users so processes can be refined rather than a big bang change to all users.

Anytime you add new tech to a process or change it, make sure you communicate those changes to the people involved.

We can't overstate how important this is.

According to Colleen, "Ask any consultant, and they will tell you that after rolling out the software, the majority of calls on a help desk are largely users asking questions related to training and understanding the new process." Your communication also needs to be in an appropriate form for the users, or they won't adopt it. Here at FloQast, we recently rolled out Coupa, but our rollout was less than perfect, in part because, as Colleen said, "accountants do not understand the value of communication."

While the accounting team did put out detailed instructions, they were in the form of a 45-page PDF that didn't even have links from the table of contents to the separate sections. What would have been more useful to someone like Colleen, who uses this tool maybe once or twice a year, would have been a flowchart that provided enough information for her to quickly use it and be done with it, instead of trying to remember the 45-page document she read six months ago.

With tools like Loom, it's easy to shoot a quick video that demonstrates new processes or tools, catering to team members who are more visual learners. Flowcharts that show the dependencies that aren't always obvious from checklists also are helpful.

When processes break down, it's usually a breakdown in either perception or communication. As we described in Chapter 7, Stefan believes that 90% of all business issues boil down to these two issues. Perception issues arise when people don't understand the overall picture of who needs what, why they need it, when they need it, and where the data should be stored. Communication issues happen when people fail to abruptly communicate potential issues with the data, or to effectively communicate to people what the overall workflow is. For example, it's vital to communicate to those downstream that the output of a process is good to go, or if there are potential issues with it. Our rollout of Coupa is another example of a failure in communication.

Communication also needs to be accessible to be effective. Make sure as you automate that everyone knows what part or parts of the new process they are responsible for. Also make sure everyone has an understanding of how their part fits into the overall plan.

STEP 3: TRACK AND MANAGE

Now that you have the separate tasks and automations documented, it's time to assign the work and track completion so you can start executing on your playbook. Ideally, this should go in a workflow tool like FloQast because managing by spreadsheet or daily status meetings becomes inefficient and unwieldy as your operations expand. If you have a tool like FloQast, it's easy to both track and manage the many processes, and to move tasks around to even out workloads. It's also easy to monitor the quality and timeliness of the work your team is doing, as well as to make sure the work is being reviewed on time.

A lot of operations is workload management for the team. Within every department, you have the All Stars — the people who work a ton and take on a lot of work, and execute flawlessly. Then you have those who work for two hours a day, and then look at ESPN or find some other way to screw around the rest of the day. And that's because the workload is not appropriately balanced in most functions. It's particularly true in accounting, which is a shame because a lot of those skills are pretty interchangeable across the different functions within the office of the CFO. So, managing the workload is a big deal for operations. Making sure the work is evenly distributed across the team allows you to work most efficiently.

Recall our definition of operationalizing: "*measuring the abstract and tracking it with the intention of improvement.*" You're not tracking and managing every little nuance of every workflow, but just the things you intend to change.

You may be tempted to move quickly into the next step of **Analyze and Optimize,** but remember that it may take a few cycles through for everyone to learn the new workflow, especially if there have been big changes from the previous iteration. You have to execute on the new workflow a few times to really know what went well and what isn't going well. Let it simmer and then ruminate on the experience. By using tech to track the processes, you collect neutral data for analysis in the next step.

STEP 4: ANALYZE AND OPTIMIZE

"Practice does not make perfect. Only perfect practice makes perfect."
-Vince Lombardi

No matter how well you document and automate your processes, things rarely work out exactly as planned. So after you've been through the new process enough times for people to learn the new workflow, you enter the Analyze and Optimize phase. Here, you essentially do a post mortem on your processes and the data you tracked to see what you can learn. Is the new process working or not? Did people understand what they were supposed to do? What can we learn from this? If it's not working, what can we do to fix it? Are there tweaks we can make to improve it? Remember, you can't fix the whole thing at once, so choose the biggest pain points to optimize.

Some organizations pick one process or area to optimize at a deep level once a month or once a quarter. It depends on how big your pain points are. If you have small ones, fixing them allows you to make progress and it won't be too bad. But if you have bigger problems, it might take a few months to get those figured out and get people on board with those changes.

You can parse out selection of the processes to optimize to your team and to the people you did walk-throughs with. You'll have much better success with analyzing and optimizing if you make sure all stakeholders have a voice. Ask them what went well, and what didn't go well. What were your biggest pain points? Are there things we can fix? Are there things we can do better? Start with the processes with the biggest potential wins, and as soon as people see you're genuinely interested in making their jobs better, you'll have much more success in getting people on board when you make changes.

It's vitally important as you optimize processes that you don't just look at your side and then "throw something over the fence," says Dante Giannini. "Now you're just crushing somebody on the other side." You need to support the others in the organization, and "make sure that everything's good, that the work is being distributed equally, and nobody's getting crushed because, 'Hey, I finished my job here.'"

Dante says in his work, he's pushing everybody on "making sure they understand all the critical touch points beyond just themselves," because "in today's world, you really need to understand how everything is flowing and fitting together, where your risk points are, how you address them and how you make sure that everybody who's working at your company is trying to do the best they can." It's the attention to the broader organization that sets the operational accountant apart from the rest.

Accountants are already good at iterating and optimizing from the close. You've likely already built a skill set around making the close faster and better, so it's not much of a leap to deploy that skill set across the broader organization. Most non-accountants don't really work, think or look at processes that way, but as accountants we can take our very structured approach and layer that on the broader organization where appropriate.

Optimizing processes means that you can't get too attached or protective of your work product. Jonathan Hardy tells his co-workers "chances are, there's a better way to do it," even if he was the one who built the process. "And I will take zero offense if you change it completely and make it better," he says. He views each process improvement as temporary, and encourages his team members to explore completely different approaches than his if that new way can save additional time.

If you see that a process fails once, don't freak out. It's part of the nature of the animal kingdom to remember and avoid things that hurt and cause scars. Confirmation bias can cause us to overreact when it was really just bad luck on that one day that caused the failure.

But by analyzing the data from the tech we use to track processes, we can see how many times the process failed. Is it failing a lot? Or did it fail just once out of many times, but that one failure was really painful? Tracking the process means you can distinguish between one day of bad luck, when maybe the person responsible was sick, or a cycle where sales really messed up the things that they usually get right, versus a more systemic failure.

That one failure might change the way you go about the process. However, maybe you don't need to throw the whole process out, but just make a little tweak so that if it fails again, it's not so painful. Maybe you don't need a reactionary control that creates a significant amount of busy work for people, and bogs the organization down, but maybe just a small control and a few changes will be sufficient.

You also want to be alert for small things that keep failing, but it's not a big deal in a given cycle that they fail. It's just an annoyance. Over time, these small bleeds can end up costing your company a lot, and can become material problems.

It used to be that auditors would look for big errors. But that slow bleed can add up over time without ever rising to the level of materiality in any one year. These days, because of audit failures, the SEC and PCAOB are asking auditors to look for these small bleed type issues. Companies applying Six Sigma also are paying attention to these small issues.

The Analyze phase isn't just about looking at the speed and

accuracy of processes. This is also the time where you can look at reporting issues. This can be as simple as looking to see if transactions are flowing correctly from record to report. You can also do some analytics to check on whether the relationships between financial statement items make sense. If they don't, be sure to look into that and try to resolve it before your next audit. By the way, if you have great auditors, they may be able to help you with this.

Another reporting issue that we tend to overlook is to ask the users of those reports what they need, whether that use is regulatory GAAP reporting or internal management. If there are issues with the usefulness or usability of those reports, is that a process issue, or is it a perception issue of what the user really needs? Or maybe it's a data issue?

Then you work on solving the issues. When we understand what the users really need, we can provide it. Accountants get so focused on the reporting side of it that we forget that the users, whether it's finance or investors, don't think like us.

Unless they're accountants, they don't always understand the intricacies of a cash flow statement. While they may grasp the big picture — that operationally, a company is net positive or net negative on cash, and that the company is investing money and financing operations, but they can't always discern the details. While we accountants may think the cash flow statement is great and provides many details of operations, if most financial statement users don't look at it or don't use it, are we really providing the report they need? Or am I doing a hard, technical accounting thing, and it's not assisting users at all?

The basic financials show that revenue went up or down, and that profits likewise went up or down. And AI tools can help us glean insights that the human eye can't easily see. But without the human element that can explain why those numbers went up or down, or the skepticism drilled into us as accountants, our understanding of what the issue really is will be limited. Our human understanding also helps us to identify the feasible solutions to those issues.

Now we're not saying that the users of financial statements don't have some responsibility in their ability to understand financials. We think that many in the finance profession and most investors need to have better accounting knowledge to be able to leverage financials better. There's a ton of information embedded in them if you understand the intricacies and the nuances of the accounting rules behind how they're created.

Maybe for internal users or investors it would be better to provide KPIs and progress toward your company-wide goals with some benchmarks or ratios that can be understood as a definition of financial health.

Are the users of GAAP financials really getting the information they need? This is where ESG reporting is coming in. There are clearly users out there who want this information. It's not just climate, but some investors are really interested in whether a company's mission and vision is tied to their financial reports. It's not easy to tell from GAAP financials whether a company's profit is related to executing on their vision. Many investors see that businesses that truly align their mission and vision to their operations are successful, resilient, and innovative. But it's hard to tell from the outside if a company is being truly honest in their claims.

Right now, the climate is one of the big drivers toward better reporting, but in 10 years, if everyone is reporting on environmental impact, investors won't stop there. They'll want to know how companies are driving diversity and inclusion. Eventually, when those drivers that make people want to change in those areas become less relevant, investors will return to the essence, which is understanding how a company is performing against their stated mission and vision.

THE CRUCIAL ROLE OF TECHNOLOGY IN YOUR PLAYBOOK

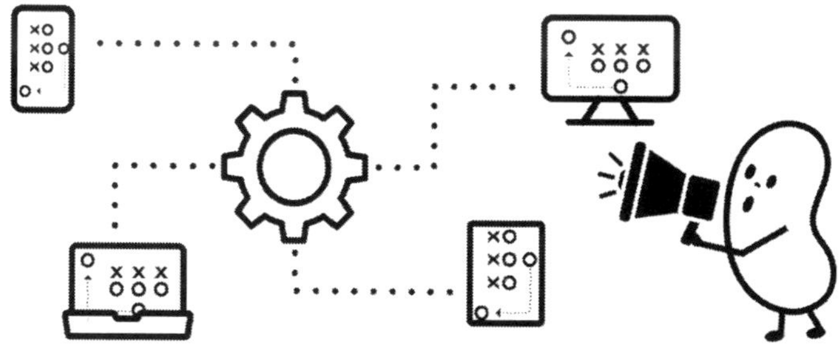

You can be a lone wolf and still be an effective operational accountant, as Stefan was at Skullcandy. But when you get the entire organization aligned around its mission and vision, when everyone sees clearly what they need to do and how it relates to the whole, then your impact can be immense. You're changing the culture of accounting especially, and causing the entire organization to be more operationally focused. And that requires using technology for effective communication.

You need to get the entire organization on the same page, and you can't do that without leveraging technology to break down silos and transform what was one-to-one and many-to-many communication into a single one-to-many repository of information.

Think of the game telephone. One person says something to one person, and when it's just two people it's fine. But then when you add other people, the message inevitably becomes garbled. Expand that to an entire organization, and information gets passed around like a spiderweb, to people above, below, behind, and in both directions, and to people who may not really understand the information before they pass it on to someone else. With this model, communication isn't timely, it's rarely effective, and it can be of questionable accuracy.

But with technology, you can communicate effectively on a

one-to-many basis when you put your playbook on a tech platform (like FloQast, for example) that everyone has individualized access to. A single central data repository ensures the information is accurate and timely. By adding customizable views, users have ready access to exactly what they need to see how their part of the organization is functioning, to the tasks they need to act on, and how they are performing against their personal objectives.

Using a tool that's quick and easy to update ensures that the information is timely and relevant. It's not out of date, as it often is when checklists are kept solely in Excel. It also lets you leverage the power of a feedback loop, where each iteration gets smoother, faster, and more effective.

INTEGRATED TECHNOLOGY SOLUTIONS MAKE EVERYTHING BETTER

As we mentioned in the introduction, FloQast has been surveying accountants about their work, seeking data to validate what we believe and what we've seen among FloQast customers. From the surveys we performed in 2022 and 2023 with the University of Georgia's Consumer Analytics program, we learned that it's not just the technology accountants use that matters, but the relationship they have with that technology that makes the biggest difference. As we mentioned briefly above, accountants tend to split into three distinct types of relationships with their technology, with about a third of accountants in each group. Here's how we describe those three groups in Chapter 2 of our Guidebook Series:[2]

> *First, there is the* ***Adversarial*** *relationship in which the technology is seen as a hindrance rather than a resource. The accountant experiences a mix of acceptance and dread knowing they are forced to use the technology. It doesn't func-*

tion the way the accountant needs or in a way that guiding principles require. ***The accountant must find ways to manipulate the technology or perform redundant work to ensure the job gets done.***

Second, there is the ***Routine*** *relationship in which the technology works but adds minimal value. It might encourage the accounting professional to take a basic or functional approach to their job or — conversely — force them to be creative, independent of the prime directive of the technology.* ***The accountant can think like the technology, but the technology cannot think like the modern accountant.***

Finally, there is the ***Synergistic*** *relationship in which the technology becomes an extension of the accountant.* ***In this relationship, it becomes difficult to tell where the accountant's efforts end and the technology's efforts begin.*** *The technology (or, more correctly, the people who designed the technology) has an intimate understanding of how accountants think and work and supports what the accountant is trying to achieve. The accountant benefits from having a true partner in their work.*

In that same survey, we also asked accountants about the degree of integration they had in their tech. We had an inkling that the more integrated the software, the better it would be for accountants. From those survey results, we found accounting tech fell into three overall buckets of low, medium, and high degrees of integration. Perhaps not surprisingly, over half (58%) of the accountants working with a highly integrated system reported a synergistic relationship with their tech, as the diagram below shows. The remaining 42% using highly integrated systems had a routine relationship with their technology. The accountants with adversarial relationships were all using tech with either a low or medium degree of integration.

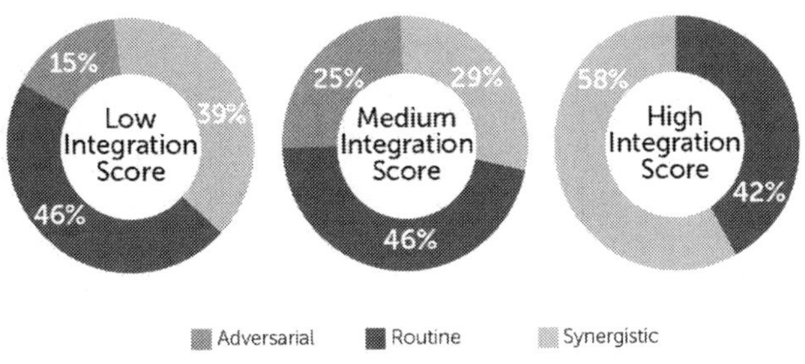

This finding that 42% of accountants using highly integrated technology still have routine relationships with their tech suggests that while it's helpful to have a highly integrated system, that's not enough to make someone feel that their tech is a partner to their work. Now we don't know absolutely for sure, but we would bet that many of those accountants with the synergistic relationship who work with highly integrated tech are using what we described back in Chapter 8 as **integrated technology solutions.**

As a reminder, an integrated technology solution not only integrates all the tech you need to do your work, but it does so in a way that allows you to work the way you think and the way you like to work, and all in a seamless and intuitive workplace. Your tech fits you like a glove. You can still use Excel and email and Slack alongside your ERP and all the other modules you need, but in a way that makes the total more than the sum of its parts. Transitioning between the tools doesn't interrupt your process because your entire business work ecosystem is integrated and shares data. It pulls the data when you need it and pushes it to where you need it. Your technology is less a tool to do the work and more a synergistic ally that enables you to perform at your best.

In contrast, an **integrated technology system,** which is what many organizations use, doesn't always consider the needs of accountants or the need to create an intuitive and satisfying user experience to enable accountants to do their jobs better. We suspect that a number of those accountants in our survey who said they were using highly integrated tech yet still had a routine relationship with that tech are stuck here. They can see the holy grail of how great it can be to work with a solution rather than a system, but can't get there with their current setup. It's that final 10% or even 5% better that is so elusive.

Another interesting finding from this research is that as integration increased from low to medium, the percentage of accountants reporting an adversarial relationship with their technology increased, from 15% to 25%. We don't have any data that explains this bump, so we can only speculate about the reasons.

One possible theory is that when the software is at a low level of integration in their software, users don't expect much, so they're not as frustrated by the limitations of their tech. The workarounds and manual parts of the work are just what you do. But as the degree of integration increases, the expectations for the software also rise. When users have the expectation that the software can do something and it doesn't, they experience what we call the failed promise of technology. We think their frustration might be what's stripping away from potentially having a more routine relationship with their technology.

An example Stefan uses to point out the ways that tech isn't always designed to think like accountants do is the deficiencies in the depreciation and amortization calculations performed by most ERPs. Say you have an asset that you want to depreciate over seven years. Most ERPs will calculate the monthly depreciation expense as the cost divided by seven, then divided by 12. Superficially, it looks correct.

But if you need to change the useful life or the value of the asset, or if you sell the asset, even though most ERPs have a mechanism for doing that, it's extremely rare that the journal entries are calculated correctly by the ERP. Why? Because it simply applies a rate and doesn't perform the calculations to create a depreciation or amortization table for the asset. When the asset needs to be adjusted for revaluation or updated for a different useful life, the ERP doesn't maintain the needed structure to apply the updates, leaving errors in the system. So then when the auditors look at it, they beat you up because it's not calculating correctly.

Figuring out these deficiencies with your ERP or point solutions is difficult. Stefan has personally spent hundreds if not thousands of hours in exploratory calls with vendors and with his IT staff on this. It's a big blind spot for accountants when they don't understand that their ERP doesn't solve the problem the way accounting does. You might be surprised at how often your ERP and your point solutions do not actually do that.

Moving from an integrated technology system to an integrated technology solution requires a mindset shift away from just a focus on the technology to a focus on the relationship between the accountant and the technology, as the diagram below shows.

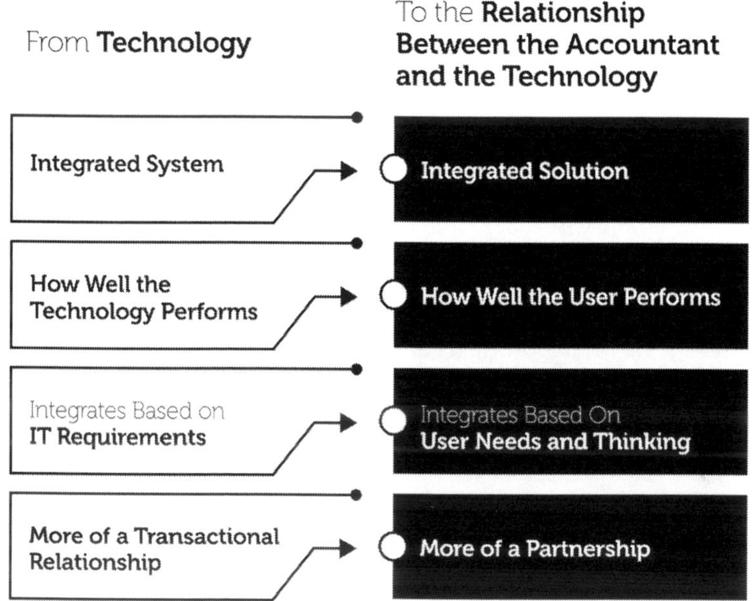

An integrated tech solution doesn't just help at the level of transactions, but helps you manage from a workflow point of view. It meets you where you're at. It's not that everything is under one roof or in one platform, but transitioning between modules or tools is seamless and intuitive. Moving between your ERP and Excel or Slack, for example, is more like putting down your fork and picking up your drink to take a sip at a meal.

Why should accountants care about this fine distinction? After all, for centuries, accountants managed just fine with paper ledgers and then for decades with awkward and temperamental computer systems. Why is it so important to work with tech that enables accountants to have a synergistic relationship with the tools of their trade?

In our research for the Controller's Guidebook series, we found that having a synergistic relationship with technology has cascading effects in nearly all areas of accountants' lives. It impacts your entire persona. Accountants who had a synergistic relationship with their tech were more likely to:

- Experience less burnout
- Believe they have enough time to complete their work
- Feel personally competent to do the work
- Have a voice within their organizations
- Be more optimistic about their career potential
- Be more satisfied with their income
- Have a better work/life balance
- Reopen the books less frequently
- Experience less disruption to their personal lives

These are all things that make life as an accountant better, more fulfilling, and more sustainable. Real accountants are achieving these things. It's not a pipe dream.

We would also say that having a synergistic relationship with your tech is essential to the Ops approach. It helps you set a baseline for getting the work done faster and more accurately so you have the bandwidth to have a voice in your organization and to do more of the strategic work all of us want to do more of. It lets you be the Lionel Messi of your organization, with a wide perception of what's happening across your organization. You're no longer running to put out fires every day, but you're able to see where you need to be to prevent the fires from even starting.

But what if you're trapped — at least momentarily — with tech that isn't at the holy grail level of an integrated technology solution? Does this mean you're necessarily going to have an adversarial or, at best, a routine relationship with your tech? Not at all, according to the accountants we surveyed.

If you take a look at the figure above that shows the correlation of integration scores and technology relationships, you can see that 15% of the accountants working with systems with a low integration score and 25% of those working with systems with a medium integration score still managed to have a synergistic relationship with their technology.

So, yes, the overall design of the tech matters a lot (if it didn't, we never would have bothered creating FloQast). But this data implies that a synergistic relationship can also be cultivated by the accountant, even if you're using less-than-optimal tech. Maybe there's some extra training or extra skills that will help fill in the gap. Or maybe it's a mindset shift you can make. Maybe you can find someone using the same or similar tech who can help you get over the hump. Or maybe if you can find a way to optimize a clunky process or workbook you inherited, you can make it better.

THE THREE PARTS OF OPS

If you recall, back in Chapter 3, we defined Ops as three things: data integrity, transactional workflow, and the overall operating cadence of the organization. In this chapter, we focused on the things you can do to optimize transactional workflow, and the importance of identifying and fixing those small bleeds that can jeopardize data integrity. Using highly integrated technology that's designed and implemented to ensure that data flows through the system from record to report accurately, and that everyone across the organization is tapping into that single source of truth, are the essential underpinnings of data integrity.

The third part of Ops is applying the accountant's discipline around deadlines to the organization as a whole, and getting all the workflows synchronized together — and that will be the focus of our next chapter.

11 / ESTABLISHING A CADENCE TO YOUR WORKFLOW

The Ops mentality means you are in a proactive state. You're no longer executing reactively, but because you have operationalized everything, and have defined the cadence, your organization is acting like an army, not just as random individuals, and everyone is pushing toward success.

THE CADENCE

To say that controllers are familiar with the monthly, quarterly, and annual cadence within accounting is an understatement. We also understand that sales operates on a similar cadence with the same regular deadlines. But not everyone (and that includes us) takes the extra step to establish a recurring cadence for product and marketing. The Cadence is a blueprint for synchronizing all the parts of a company so that everything is working from the same overall playbook.

It was a lightbulb moment for Mike when he first heard David Sacks talk about The Cadence.[1] David Sacks learned about The Cadence when he was COO at PayPal, and applied this process as CEO and founder of Yammer. Before being acquired by Microsoft for $1.2 billion in 2012, David scaled Yammer to 500 employees and $56 million in annual sales in just four years.

EVERYTHING IN SYNC, EVERY QUARTER

With The Cadence, every department's calendar is in sync: Product launches something every quarter. Marketing gets the word out about the new release with content and press releases, and produces the sales collateral that the reps use to educate customers. Sales focuses on hitting their quarterly targets for each launch. Finance and the office of the CFO track and report on the numbers. The Cadence is how you get the whole company on deadline, getting things done.

This all starts with planning between sales and finance. These two teams work closely together on the same calendar. The other side of the equation is product and marketing, with their own quarterly calendar, which is offset by six weeks within the quarter so that product has a new release at the midpoint of every calendar quarter.

Every quarter, there's something new coming out. Maybe it's an upgrade to an existing product, or maybe it's a new feature or even a completely new offering. The idea is to keep momentum going by reengaging prospects or bringing new leads into the marketing funnel. Marketing creates the awareness and excitement around that new release to generate sales. In the appendix, FloQast's former Director of Product Marketing, Colleen Wanty, will explain a widely used framework that we use.

David created The Cadence for SaaS companies, and it works well for organizations that have regular updates and upgrades and new products. Not every organization has the right business model to perfectly align all these calendars, but we encourage you to think through this model and see what parts of it you can bring to your organization.

The benefit of having a regular mid-quarter cadence around product and marketing is that your sales team will be in a position to sell more effectively at the end of the quarter. That requires your product marketing and sales enablement teams to be locked at the hip so they can get the training done by week six. If you can't do that, you risk hurting your numbers the rest of the quarter, and you may not hit your numbers for the quarter. The Cadence doesn't make your sales team more efficient, or teach them to negotiate better. But getting all the pieces aligned helps the sales team to be more effective at their jobs because they have the sales materials and the knowledge about the latest product release they need.

If Product will be launching something new in week six, then starting by week one, product marketing will be producing collateral then handing it off to sales enablement. Sales enablement will work closely with sales to ensure the sales team is getting trained up on the new product or new features. That may include creating the content pieces that sales needs to talk to customers. Product marketing will also be producing white papers. Similarly, over in product, you have to get the offering and the pricing lined up.

WHO'S IN CHARGE OF THE CADENCE?

While the CEO may set the quarterly and annual roadmap, someone has to be in charge of making sure everything happens in the correct cadence. And in Mike's opinion — and the opinion of plenty of other high-achieving company leaders — the CFO is the logical one to do this. And because the CFO inevitably has too much on his or her plate, much of that responsibility will inevitably land on the controller. And the best controllers for the job are those with the Ops mindset.

The finance team and the office of the CFO are the ones with access to the data, and the ability to analyze and interpret the data, so they are the obvious choice to be in charge of The Cadence. The company accountants already work with all the other departments in some capacity. We prepare the commission statements for sales and pay payroll for them. We collaborate with marketing to get information for accruals. We provide marketing and product with budget information so they can do their job better. By working with each department, we have at least a high level of understanding of what everyone is doing and the workflows they follow to get their work done. When we document those workflows, we can help to optimize them and keep that cadence in place.

OUR START WITH THE CADENCE

FloQast started with a quarterly cadence for sales and accounting. We had quarterly goals that we tracked against. We closed the books every month and every quarter and had quarterly financials which we presented to the board. It felt like normal stuff to Mike, since he'd come from a company where that was the way the accounting was done.

To stay on top of sales goals, we send out what we call a "banana chart" every week to all the employees and investors. This chart shows the cumulative recurring revenue we add each week to show the progress we're making toward quarterly sales goals. We call it a "banana chart" because progress isn't a straight line, but is generally curved, with the steepest part at the end of the quarter, when the pressure is on to hit our goal. Interestingly, the sales team generally doesn't have problems hitting deadlines and getting deals done on time. But that's likely because their commissions are on the line. They're selfishly motivated to grind and hit their numbers.

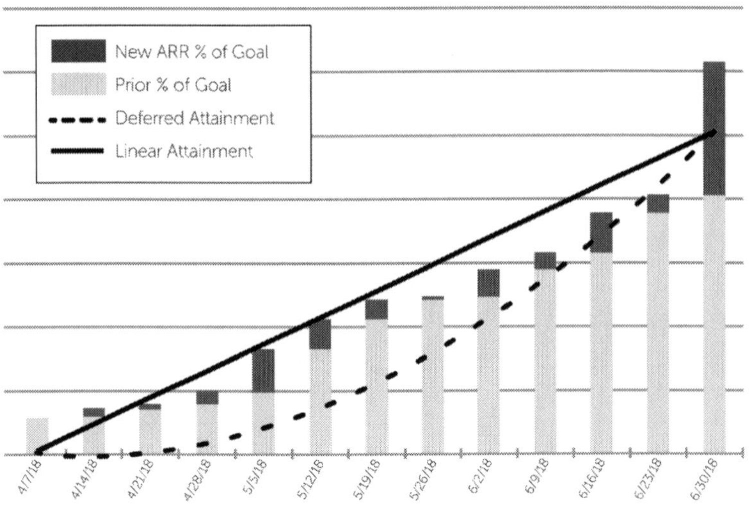

But not all startups operate that way, so a lot of them just get shaken out. To Mike, it just makes common sense to keep finance and sales on track. You have quarterly goals you want to hit every quarter, and we track that with our banana chart.

The Cadence brings in the notion that product and marketing are the functions that support your company in hitting those quarterly numbers. This quarterly cadence for product and marketing is something that's not really understood by accountants. This was a new idea for Mike when he first heard it. And, as Colleen explains in the Appendix, product and marketing aren't always on a quarterly timeline. But if you do put it on a quarterly timeline, then, like the cadence for finance and accounting, it's all deadlines.

Now at FloQast, we're not the best example of a product and marketing cadence by any stretch of the imagination. We've had a quarter where we had two massive product announcements, and nothing for three quarters before that. But there are things you can work backward from.

Getting product launches out by deadline is a battle that Mike has had with Cullen since day one. Over in engineering, they'll say, "Well, things go wrong. What if this is harder than we thought and there's a bug, and we miss our deadline by two weeks?" But things like that happen in accounting all the time. Maybe you just acquired a company, or a new piece of guidance comes out, or the auditors find something. We can't just go to the CFO and ask for another two weeks to close the books. We're going to make miracles happen to get it done. It's non-negotiable. If we miss the deadline, the bank might call a note. The company might shut down. We work together to help the team.

HITTING DEADLINES IS OUR SUPERPOWER

Deadlines are something that we as accountants know how to hit because our deadlines are non-negotiable. It's in our DNA to attack deadlines operationally and work backward to figure out what needs to happen by when to hit that deliverable deadline. We would both say that accountants are best ones for holding marketing and product accountable for getting their work done on a quarterly basis the same way the CFO and the controller holds finance and sales responsible for getting their work done on a quarterly basis.

There's a bit of a difference between the deadlines for accounting and for sales, product and marketing. For accounting, people want the financials faster, so they want to accelerate the deadline, which happens after the quarter ends. You're always trying to close faster so the deadline ideally is getting closer to the end of the quarter.

But for the other areas of the organization, the deadline is always the end of the quarter. You're not looking to end the quarter faster for sales. But what the Ops person can do is identify efficiencies within the quarter, so you still hit your number, but without wasting as much time or effort.

With these other areas it's about driving profitability and helping with ROI. It's not about getting it done faster — like it is when you're trying to close faster — but about getting it done more efficiently. It's a slightly different twist than the expectations we have as accountants.

Stefan says it's the DNA of accountants that we iterate our processes to improve them constantly. It's what we do with the close. But until we insert ourselves into operations as an operational accountant, the rest of the organization doesn't generally have that mindset of iteration and optimization to the cadence they follow. In the forward-thinking organizations we work with, we see clearly that the accountants who fully embrace the Ops mentality are the catalyst for driving changes across their organizations.

It doesn't matter what you're doing, whether it's marketing, sales, or even creating new and unique deliverables; there should be a way to operationalize and put a cadence to what you're doing. The highest state of execution is having an understanding of what your business cadence is, and executing to that cadence. You're responding to challenges proactively as they arise, not reacting retroactively as most businesses do.

ACT AS AN ARMY, MOVING IN SYNC

The Ops approach is all about getting everything and everyone in the organization focused and moving forward, continually iterating and improving. When you put a cadence to your operations so that everything is aligned around the company goals, you're acting as an army, not as a group of random individuals contributing to something that no one fully understands. You're moving together, in harmony, toward those goals. Outside of sales and accounting, most other areas tend to have a casual attitude about deadlines. But when the controller applies a cadence to operations, you're countering that attitude with the discipline of an operational accountant.

There's something magical that happens when leadership puts out clear, tangible goals on a regular cadence. When David Sacks was at Yammer, product was expected to put out something new every quarter. A tangible goal like that gives everyone something to work toward. When you put tangible goals in front of people, that can inspire incredible, almost heroic efforts. People find they are able to achieve levels of performance they may not have believed possible. And more often than not, people do actually achieve those goals because they have a target for their actions and their intentions.

Ambiguous goals, like "increase sales" or "release upgrades a few times a year" can be much harder to achieve because it's hard to know what to focus on. They're more like the vague New Year's resolutions people make that are quickly abandoned when the going gets tough. Achieving ambiguous goals generally happens only with serendipity; by some stroke of luck, everyone did their job well and focused on the right things, and the right conditions just happened to sync up at the right time. And if you don't achieve an ambiguous goal, it's easy to dismiss that failure as just bad luck or market conditions outside everyone's control.

That's why it's better to use a goal-setting framework like the SMART method. SMART goals are:

- Specific – people know what's to be achieved, the steps to get there, and who's responsible
- Measurable – there are specific benchmarks so that everyone knows when the goal has been achieved
- Achievable – the goal is something the team can realistically achieve, not something completely out of reach
- Relevant – the goal has a connection to the North Star for the company
- Time-bound – people know the timing so they can plan their actions with the intention of achieving the goal within the specified timeframe

Achieving the goal of consistently releasing something new every quarter requires intention. Everyone across the company needs to be on board and committed to working toward that goal. The pressure to release something — a new feature, a substantial upgrade, or even an entirely new product — will summon forth everyone's creativity, vision, and imagination.

To execute dependably on that cadence, leadership and product must have a finger firmly on the pulse of the pain points of the market, while also looking to the environment to see what customers might be wanting in the future. The organization has to be constantly anticipating what that next new thing is.

As an operational accountant, you can play a key role in

seeking out that next new thing simply because you're connected to all parts of the organization. Because you have established respectful and open relationships across the company, people will be more willing to share their insights and ideas. Some ideas will be good, and some won't be. But unless someone is collecting all those ideas and sifting through them, that brilliant hunch from someone in sales or engineering will be lost.

That next new thing won't necessarily be what the customers think they need, but it may well be that thing that creates a new paradigm. There's an old story that if Henry Ford had asked people what they wanted back when he was creating the first mass-market automobiles, they would have asked for faster horses. And before Apple released the first iPhone, who would have thought anyone would want to watch videos and full-length movies on a tiny screen?

The Cadence requires organizations to always be fresh and new and moving forward. You can't be stale and sinking into oblivion when you are always reinventing and reimagining what you produce and how you serve the world.

When accounting adopts the operational approach, you're helping the leadership team find the bandwidth to envision that next new thing that guides the company closer to its North Star. Instead of constantly putting out fires and worrying about fixing the next thing that breaks, the organization is moving forward in sync. You're reducing the deadweight of operational debt so the company is leaner and more agile.

The Ops approach won't solve everything. Nothing does. There will always be unforeseen and unforeseeable jolts to the world like COVID and wars and natural disasters. Technological change is accelerating to make today's cutting-edge tech look as quaint and outdated as rotary dial phones and adding machines. But what the Ops approach helps with is creating a highly efficient and agile organization that will weather those jolts better than the organizations that haven't adopted this mindset yet.

Now that you have the foundation of the Ops approach, in the next and final part of this book we will look at the future of accounting and how operational accounting will be the key to succeeding in this brave new world.

PART 3

HOW OPS WILL TAKE OVER BUSINESS

12 / WHAT WILL ACCOUNTING LOOK LIKE IN 2050?

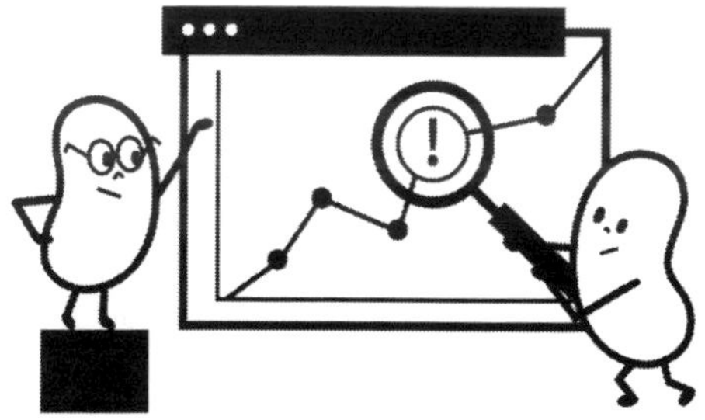

Our grand vision is that by 2050, most COOs will have come up through accounting. Within the next 26 years, accounting will become the center of every organization. The Ops approach we've laid out in this book is the way we get there. But first, let's make a slight detour and think about the possibilities of what accounting will be like in 2050.

WHAT WILL ACCOUNTING LOOK LIKE IN 2050?

Like most accountants, we've spent a good chunk of our careers focused on the rearview mirror of the past, as reflected in the financial statements of the organizations we work at or that we audited. While looking to the road ahead through the windshield provides a much bigger and broader perspective, the horizon of the future keeps shifting, seemingly every week, as new developments in technology promise us a brilliant future while regulatory organizations continually throw up increasingly complex barriers to that promised future.

One way to think about the possibilities of technology is to think about the first cars, where just starting the car took a lot of manual processes. You had to stand in front and actually turn a crank to get it started. But today, you can get into a Tesla, and you just push a button. Not only does it start automatically, it drives you and it entertains you. You don't need to think about all the things that have to happen in between pushing the button and reaching your destination.

It will be the same thing in accounting. Eventually, you won't need to think about most of the things that happen between the transaction occurring and the reporting of that transaction in the financials and the dashboards that leaders rely on to make decisions. The output of accounting will be the individualized information that everyone in the company needs to do their job, whether it's financial data, non-financial data, or pieces of that data married together.

The Ops person is the one who's going to identify that opportunity and implement the technology to handle it. The staff accountants won't even be aware of the automation going on behind the scenes. It will just be how they do their jobs.

What about technology? Moore's Law, which is more accurately an observation and prediction than a hard and fast law,[1] says that the density of transistors in an integrated circuit will double about every 18 months to two years. Despite some voices saying that Moore's Law is dead, others, such as Intel's CEO Pat Gelsinger,[2] say it's alive and well. Futurists such as

Thomas Frey, former IBM engineer and designer, predict that AI will disrupt our lives in ways we can't imagine.[3] Frey predicts that smart contracts will one day eliminate large chunks of bureaucracy and managerial overhead.[4] It's hard for us to imagine what might be possible in a few years with quantum computing, blockchain, neural network computing, and the many developments in AI.

Just think how far accounting tech has come in the last few decades. Some on our team at FloQast remember closing the books on paper. Then the first GLs on mainframe computers came along, a huge improvement, but they were far too expensive for smaller organizations. Desktop computers and development of desktop GLs like QuickBooks and Peachtree put computerized financials in the reach of many more organizations. Cloud computing has been the next evolution. What comes next — who knows? Maybe blockchain will play a role, maybe we'll have something as unimaginable as the first iPhones were before they came on the market in 2007.

So what will accounting look like in 2050? If Moore's Law continues to play out and if the futurists are right, by 2050 (just 26 years from now), we will likely see changes in accounting tech that we can't imagine. As a point of reference, it was only 26 years ago (in 1998) that the first version of QuickBooks was released. Our favorite tool — the spreadsheet — is only 20 years older than that, with the development of VisiCalc, which led to Lotus 1-2-3 in 1983 and Excel in 1985. The first cellphone call was made in 1973, with a phone the size of a brick.[5] Today, cellphones are an indispensable part of our daily lives.

To answer this, we asked a few forward-thinking accountants what they think the future will look like. Of course, Stefan and Mike chime in occasionally. We consulted:

- Jerry Raphael, CFO of Hypori
- Jonathan Hardy, Director of FP&A at LeadVenture
- Greg Vecellio, Controller at FloQast
- Razzak Jallow, CFO of FloQast
- Hugh O'Neill, Sales Engineering Manager at FloQast

AUTOMATION WILL TAKE CARE OF THE ROTE PARTS OF OUR JOBS

Advances in tech won't take our jobs away, but they will change it, as every other advance in accounting tech has done. "We would have thought when we replace the abacus with the pen and paper, or replace the pen and paper with Excel that everybody would have to be gone," says Hugh O'Neill. "But there's still a lot of people doing accounting even though everything is digitized. It'll just be a different type of work."

Jerry Raphael agrees that we'll have different kinds of work. While "there are jobs being lost to automation every day of the week, there are also new jobs being created." Jerry points to the position of revenue accountant, which has been in every organization he's worked in for the last three years, but which didn't exist a decade ago, not until the complexities of ASC 606 kicked in. Who knows what the next big complex standard from FASB and IASB will be, but we can be sure there will be something.

By 2050, "a lot of the stuff we spend time on today should be automated," says Jonathan Hardy, even some of the more challenging work, such as vendor accruals. "There is no reason why eventually technology can't do that," he says. By then, Jonathan believes that we will have AI tools that will evaluate the spending trends in various areas over the previous several months to come up with a reasonable accrual, a task that currently takes one of his team members two full days to do every close cycle.

When the debits and credits are automated, Jonathan believes that the work will be more analytical, blurring the line between accounting and FP&A work. "It will be more of making sure that the story makes sense and that the numbers that the AI is producing match our expectations." Jonathan believes that by 2050, the routine monthly work will be fully automated, and accounting departments will not require the headcount needed today.

Jerry agrees that accounting departments will likely shrink. "When you can connect all the dots, the individual jobs that people are doing now can be consolidated around a few automations. So maybe you don't need three people to do it, and now you only need one." Organizations themselves may not be leaner, but roles within those organizations will be completely different.

Just as we who have grown up using computers to do our work can't imagine doing accounting with paper ledgers, the next generation will not be able to conceive of the many manual tasks we still need to do today. It's a given, according to Greg Vecellio, that AI and automation will "eliminate the grunt work." The work that doesn't help with career growth and doesn't excite us, but just has to get done.

Although tech today automates many of the steps, many of the tools still require someone to actually pull the data from the bank or from the GL. Greg envisions a future where "that's completely automated, and at a certain date, a bot will request the general ledger data and the bank data. It just happens without anyone having to do anything, and then someone reviews it."

Many things that aren't automated today will be in the

future, according to Jerry, who sees the progress of automation as part of a continuum. Tasks like billing and rev rec used to have to run manually, but now we have tools that can do that for us, even though not everyone is using those tools today.

TECHNOLOGY FOR DEEPER VISIBILITY

Eliminating these kinds of rote tasks will give people the mental bandwidth to focus on more challenging and higher level work so that people take the time to think about their work instead of rushing through it to get to the next step. Controllers will be more like Lionel Messi; they will have deeper visibility, with a deeper understanding of their organization, and not working as much or as frantically as many do today. Instead, they will be working strategically, intentionally, to create opportunity.

Because everyone is focused on the rote tasks before them that need to get done, Greg often sees team members rushing through work so they can move on to the next item on their to-do list. But the step they skip is asking themselves "Is this even right to begin with?" Greg hopes that by eliminating the rote tasks, team members will have more bandwidth to think about their work, and that by "removing the task mindset, you free them to start thinking more critically, which then makes every decision better." That critical thinking includes thinking about whether a particular task even makes sense to do.

Jerry Raphael envisions "a way of communicating without using any form of paper or even email, where all the systems are connected and talk to each other." Jerry sees some of this today with AP automation, where "a ton of companies have married up the entire process from bank, GL, payments, credit cards, employee expenses, and they've made it seamless across the board." Connecting all the data is the first step to setting up custom access to data so that companies can send the appropriate information to interested parties when they need it, whether it's the government, investors, employees or anyone else, according to their access level and specific requirements, without forcing someone at the company to create or run a custom report or series of reports.

Stefan sees future technology that fully supports the Ops approach and the new ways that people will work in the future. The future of work will be asynchronistic operations, with people doing the work on their schedule and updating results as they do it. To support that, he envisions an operations-focused tech platform — perhaps an advanced version of what we are building with FloQast Ops — that "painlessly captures and reports the tribal knowledge that exists across the organization, including all the boots-on-the-ground, line-of-sight perspectives, and communicates that information effectively throughout the organization. People will no longer have to go searching for that information and will be able to make better decisions throughout the organization. Everyone will have an increased perception of what's actually happening." In Stefan's perfect vision for this tool, updating it won't be a burden because it's built into the processes, and the tool itself will dynamically update with a checklist of things each team member needs to get done each day.

In Stefan's conception, this tool won't be just a one-way demand for action on lower team members but also will be integrated seamlessly into the FP&A tools used to track progress toward organizational goals. "It will be an early warning sign when things go wrong, sort of like an advanced home security system that warns of problems like leaks or fire hazards before they become full-fledged disasters. You're not waiting for your basement to fill with sewage before you call the plumber and you're not coming home to a burned-out house."

So, for example, if the plan was to build 100 widgets during the month, but on the 10th, someone in production updates that to 80, then the finance team has an early warning that the revenue projection won't be met. Someone from finance can check with production to find out what the issue is, and maybe fix it, or adjust the budget accordingly. "It's way better than getting to the end of the month and finding out after the fact, and then having to explain to the board what happened," Stefan says. "You can be forward thinking and adapt on your feet to salvage the situation."

SERVING OUR ORGANIZATIONS AT A DEEPER LEVEL

With that deeper visibility, and less time spent on purely rote tasks, Mike wants to see that accountants can pick their heads up, and are "able to work across the organization holistically and understand every function and then take your skill set as a process-oriented, detail-focused person and apply that across the whole organization to make it that much better."

Jonathan Hardy points to the time savings when automation does more. Today, accountants spend "a lot of time putting the numbers together and then we spend a lot of time trying to understand the numbers. If you don't have to put them together, then you can spend the majority of your time understanding them." This will allow accountants to have deeper conversations with the board, the executive team and the auditors. "People will know more about what's going on in the business rather than just knowing what the number is," he says.

This deeper visibility into an organization and additional capacity from automation also means that a controller or CFO of a large company can have the kind of experience that Hugh

O'Neill had when he worked at a small company, where he was "a bit of a Swiss Army knife," troubleshooting and resolving whatever problems came along. Hugh's responsibilities encompassed multiple roles that larger organizations assign to different people or even different departments. "I think it'll be interesting to see what else will come into the purview of accounting as those roles and technology changes," Hugh says. He hypothesizes that AI tools like today's ChatGPT may even make it possible for a controller to ask the AI to "give me a contract to execute for sales, and give me the best version of the contract." Controllers with the operational approach are a natural fit for this Swiss Army knife role because, as Hugh says, "they tend to be pretty technologically literate, they know how systems are organized, and they know how processes work."

Deeper visibility also offers the opportunity to get the entire company aligned around the same incentives so that everyone is pushing toward the same goal, according to our CFO, Razzak Jallow. While sales and accounting are already a pretty good example of that alignment — revenue drives the value of the company, and accounting translates what's done in sales into revenue and profits — future innovation will spread this across the entire organization.

Razzak believes that the ability to crunch large amounts of disparate data and the availability of more data will lead to greater insights. "The operations leadership in the future will be a combination of not just being able to understand the different parts within the company and how they're driving value, but then to take that and quickly realize what operational processes we need to change to better align those incentives so that everyone has the same goal," he says. In contrast, today's incentives can be slightly disconnected across organizations. For example, the contract options that create the most value for a given customer may mean that under ASC 606, the revenue may not show up in the P&L for some time. Sales wants to optimize for the customer, while accounting wants to optimize for the company. Razzak suggests that accountants are best positioned to "figure out when we should build our processes around how it will show up in the P&L, and when we should build our processes around the underlying value to the customer."

Hugh says this added depth of knowledge is "about trying to make the business better and perform better." But this will depend on how willing people are to work together and how open they are to advice. "I think you'll see some enlightened teams who will use that additional capacity to do something positive. And then you'll also see some people who will say 'Get off my turf. This is my job.'" Working effectively in Ops will require controllers to find common ground between these two camps.

SOFT SKILLS WILL BECOME THE NEW POWER SKILLS

The operational approach will require accountants to collaborate with more people across the organization, but one challenge for controllers who currently want to take a more operational role is the question of how willing people are to collaborate with finance, according to Hugh. "A big challenge for finance is that we're seen as outsiders, as the enemy, or as the bean counters," he says.

Our training as auditors is generally short on collaboration and conflict resolution. But "as automation strips away what we're doing, it's going to become a more human job and a more interactive job," Hugh says. "Your influence can be around how you engage with people, how you can talk to people, and how you can manage." Relationships with others across the organization and the ability to understand the perspectives of people in different areas will be the crucial skills for success in the future.

Another crucial skill for the future is the art of storytelling. Stefan reminds us that in all the reporting we do, "it's not about the numbers, it's about the story behind the numbers. I don't do a variance analysis just to have a variance analysis. I do it to understand what actually occurred." Remember that not everyone has the nuanced understanding of the language of accounting that we've developed, so we need to be able to put the context of what happened into a story that people can understand, remember, and reflect on.

Without the context of a story, the numbers just flow aimlessly through everyone's consciousness, to be forgotten within minutes. But a story puts a marker on those numbers, and helps everyone think about what happened as a way to create change in your organization. Of course, telling a story requires you to think about those numbers so you have a story to tell. Our expectation for the future is that because controllers are using integrated technology solutions and have a synergistic relationship with their tech, they will have the bandwidth to actually think about those numbers and come up with the stories. We also can imagine a future where the AI embedded in the tech will point out the areas we need to focus on, and may even suggest stories to help us understand what happened.

WHAT ABOUT THE ROLE OF AI?

As we're finishing this book, there's been a huge amount of hype in the marketplace around the role of generative artificial intelligence in all areas of our lives. It seems like every tech company out there is putting out something that purports to be a brand-new application of AI. Some of these sound more like they're capitalizing on the current enthusiasm around

ChatGPT than actual innovative and well-thought-out uses for AI. Accountants should be aware that these new use cases might not have all the security that sensitive financial data requires, so we encourage everyone to do their own due diligence and ask the hard questions about data security and regulatory compliance.

AI has been part of the foundation of FloQast for years, happily humming along in the background, and making reconciliations faster and more accurate. We're very much in favor of using generative AI algorithms to take over more of the mundane, error-prone and boring manual tasks so that humans can do what humans do best.

But because FloQast was founded by two former auditors, and because we understand how vitally important data security is, we'll be taking a cautious and thorough approach to exploring how further use cases can benefit our customers while also keeping their data secure.

Mike says that many of today's conversations about AI and accounting tend to look at one of two extremes: "We're all going to be automated and out of a job," or "this isn't going to work." He believes that the future will land in a gray area between these two extremes. "The actual conversation should be that AI is going to automate us down to 40 hours a week; that's the perfection level." After we shake out what we really need, "AI could just be the solution to a work-life balance rather than automating all of our jobs."

AI on its own won't solve all the problems we have in accounting, and it won't really change the overall story, according to Mike. However, it might help with the ongoing talent crunch.

As Mike says, "The economy will continue to grow and capitalism will march on, and there will be more jobs and more new businesses. In many professions, it might not be a good thing that a lot of jobs might be automated. But in accounting, we need some of them to be automated."

The younger generations coming into the workplace don't have the patience or desire for the kinds of grunt work we spent the first few years of our careers doing. And there aren't enough people coming into accounting that we can afford to burn out the majority of people who start out as staff accountants. It's not likely to get any better in the future. So we will need all the secure and reliable AI tools we can find to remove the boring stuff so new people don't immediately quit, and so that accounting becomes an attractive career choice.

The great promise of AI is that it will speed up automation so we can get financial results faster. Faster access to data means business leaders can make decisions faster, more in real time. That also means faster feedback on decisions, as Jonathan explains. "If your close is automated through AI, then instead of five days, can it take two and a half days? And your CEO has the management reporting back within four days? Then they really know that this decision we made a month ago is already driving results." Though a two-and-a-half day close may seem unbelievably fast today, we expect that by 2050, tech-forward firms will find even that too slow, or perhaps that the monthly close is an artifact of the past.

Besides reducing reporting time, Jonathan sees a potential cost savings from headcount, "especially if the accounting and FP&A lines get more blurred." Cost savings might also come from advances in tech that simplify the tech stack, so that instead of bolting yet more pieces of software onto NetSuite to take care of each specific process, you could just "have one provider that does all of it, and it becomes part of the native functionality of the ERP platforms."

Mike sees that the role of the accountant going forward will be reviewing the work of AI as it tries to interpret transactions so it can book them automatically. But regulation will have to catch up. "When AI is booking transactions and doing a lot of the accounting work, where do audits fit into all of that? Will you be auditing the decisions that the AI made? How do you do that?" The SEC and PCAOB will have to get there with new regulations on documentation and audit methodology, which may take 10 or 15 years, but Mike has faith that they will eventually get there.

Jerry predicts that AI will fundamentally transform the kind of work accountants do, and sees a big impact on business even today. "The skills required to perform rote tasks are becoming less valuable in the marketplace and eventually will be taken over by AI," he says. "Accountants have to be at the forefront of this and need to embrace the change while learning new skills and finding new ways to add value to the enterprise."

While many of us may inwardly groan at the notion of having to master a whole new set of skills, Stefan believes that AI tools may be a way to elevate the abilities of new people. "I think AI is going to be able to give you the starting point for building a financial model, and you'll go in and perfect it. It's almost like it elevates you to be like the journeyman or the master electrician so you don't have to go through the apprenticeship phase. You're perfecting it instead of going in there and doing the hard work."

IF TECH DOES THE WORK, HOW DO WE LEARN ACCOUNTING?

The great promise of the automations and AI tech of the future is that the mundane work of booking journal entries, recording transactions, and reconciling accounts will now be performed largely automatically. However, it's questionable that the output of AI — at least in its current form — will be adequate as a starting point for less-experienced accountants. A prime weakness of today's versions of AI is that they lack the ability to evaluate whether the output makes sense or is even factually correct. This means that users will have to somehow acquire that base knowledge of how accounting works so they can review the output for reasonableness and make any necessary adjustments.

Without the years of grunt work we've put in, it's hard to imagine how future generations will learn how accounting works. Stefan foresees that "there's going to be a large swath of people that are going to become very incompetent at the foundational skills because that's been done for them." He likens this to the fundamental weakness in basic math skills many people today have because we rely on calculators. "When I was in third or fourth grade, I could have done this multiplication problem a lot faster. I knew the tricks to make it super fast." While he has retained enough of those math skills to easily calculate a 20% or even 18% tip in his head, he sees that "many people just throw down a number because they literally don't know how to do it, or they have to pull out their phone to do the math."

Because AI will provide us with a better calculator, an easy way to write, and easy access to research, Stefan believes that "a lot of people will lose the art of writing, lose the art of reviewing or coming up with powerful messaging because AI does such a great job of it that when they don't have access or it's not doing exactly what you want, you lose your value to the business."

However, Stefan believes that the benefits of technology far outweigh the negatives. While past generations may have been better at mental math than we are now, he says that "without tools like computers and calculators, the progress we've made overall as a society would not have been achievable. We wouldn't have any of this technology." While it would be nice if everyone were better at mental math, "Would I exchange it for the computing power we have today?" Stefan asks. "The answer is absolutely not."

Now, some of us who did go through all that might be a little bitter that the younger people today don't have to go through learning things the hard way like we did. But Stefan reminds us that we need to mentally step back and consider whether we really want others to suffer. "Why would I want this for the next generation?" he says. "The whole point of technology is so that people don't have to go through our pain, so they can have a better time in this profession. Let people have a good life."

So if the tech does all the work, how will the future generations of accountants learn what we know now? As Greg says about accounting in the future, "You're not going to be posting journal entries. Ideally, you're going to be reviewing them to see if they make sense. And in order to know if this makes sense, you've got to understand the accounting rules, but you also have to understand what's going on in the business."

Or as Hugh says, "If you're going to understand the financial systems and the technology and how a business works, you need to fundamentally understand how a business works." If the objective is to move controllers into an operational role, how will future accountants gain that understanding of "how a business works," and whether journal entries make sense if they don't spend time in the weeds?

Those of us who didn't have to learn accounting by manually entering transactions in paper subledgers, or by manually entering transactions one by one in the first computer GLs, but were able to use bank feeds and automations to bring data into the ERP still learned how transactions flow through a system. We have to let go of the idea that the way we learned accounting is the only way to learn it. Future generations will learn in a different way, but they will still learn the transaction flow.

It may feel like we're giving up something foundationally if the next generations don't have to do things the hard, manual way that we had to endure to learn mental math or even accounting. But Stefan believes "this will provide benefits that are maybe hard for us to see right now. But foundationally, society seems to function just fine."

As an example, Stefan points to the way we used to keep track of the balance in our bank accounts. It used to require the tedious process of keeping a manual balance in a check register, and then a monthly process of balancing that check register against the paper statements so we wouldn't accidentally overdraw our bank accounts. But today, people don't need to do that. "They know what their balance is every day. Transactions are automatic, so the balance online is roughly the correct balance."

The other option is to not use the technology, and then "you're stuck in the same place and you're stagnant," Stefan reminds us.

The next generations will have their own challenges and their own burdens that we have not had to deal with. They will be dealing with nonfinancial reporting in areas like ESG that we cannot even conceive of. Stefan compares it to the way that the older audit partners learned their trade. "Back in their day, they were allowed to use circular references. They didn't need nearly the amount of evidence. The financial statements were a lot easier than they are now. But," Stefan continues, "they did have to walk around with heavy bags and tie things out by hand, using red and blue and green pencils and that sounds super tedious, but it wasn't nearly as difficult intellectually as the job is today." It's not that the younger generations will necessarily have an easier time.

Things will be hard, but hard in a different way than they were for us.

One way we could help new accountants learn how accounting works would be to revamp our education system. We need colleges to be providing that part of the educational experience now, so that when someone graduates with an accounting degree, they have enough of an understanding of how to actually do accounting and leverage these tools that they'll be able to be effective in the workforce.

The need to update our education system extends across the board. "Our entire education system is 30 years behind the curve on everything," says Razzak, who has three kids in school now. "It's still 80-plus percent memorization. There are certainly some things that are foundational. You want to understand how things work. But for many things, people don't need to understand exactly how the thing works. You need to understand how to use the tool that does the thing."

For example, regression analysis can be used to help with forecasting or to understand relationships between things. "I don't need to know how to calculate a regression model," says Razzak. "I need to know how to interpret a regression model and how to have my tool do the regression for me."

Our world today is already filled with tech tools, and by 2050, we'll be depending on even more technology to do our jobs. This means that education will have to massively change. In this book, we've been advocating for people to be more strategic and more operational in their roles so they can have great jobs and great careers. "And we should be teaching them how to use the latest tools, how to be critical thinkers, and how to drive things forward operationally or strategically," Razzak continues. "Instead, we're teaching them how to memorize."

Along with learning how to use tools, our colleges and universities also need to teach people how to evaluate the strengths and weaknesses of those tools, and to learn to use new tools as they emerge, "Because whatever you learn in college, even if you learn the most modern tool, five years later, a new tool will displace it," Razzak concludes.

These days (and for the foreseeable future), accounting course content at universities and colleges is tied strongly to the content of the CPA exam. While the AICPA just revamped this content to include a greater emphasis on technology for a new exam starting in 2024, it's doubtful that this change will provide students with the technical foundation they need now and in the future. Plus, with the ever-expanding complexity of accounting standards, universities already have a hard time covering enough theory so graduates can pass the CPA exam.

Unless our education system undergoes this massive shift, the only other option is for people to be trained on the job, which is more or less the system we have now with entry-level jobs, both in industry and in public accounting. But when those positions are automated out of existence, that puts an even bigger burden on companies, which are already stretched for resources. It also makes college an even more questionable proposition when there's a huge gap between what students learn and what they need to know to do the work.

With the increasing importance of technology to accounting, maybe an accounting degree should have more computer science course requirements? Mike thinks that perhaps the 30 additional hours required to meet the 150-hour requirement should be in computer science, just to provide some baseline understanding for what will be an even more tech-focused future.

Mike thinks that AI is going to be on the level of the calculator, Excel and the cloud as a technology that will change things. "To use either a calculator or Excel, you have to first understand how numbers work and how accounting works so you can punch in the formulas to do the work," Mike says. "So maybe you'll need some basic understanding of how AI works so that when you're interacting with a chatbot or reviewing the output of AI, you'll have the computer science equivalent of understanding numbers and debits and credits."

THE CAREER PATH IS CHANGING

When Greg started out in his career, CFOs generally came up through the controller's seat. He was told that the time he spent in FP&A — away from hard accounting — automatically disqualified him for a future role as CFO. Today, that's flipped, as many CFOs are coming from FP&A. This includes our own CFO, Razzak Jallow. As we said at the beginning of this chapter, we believe that controllers who embrace the Ops approach will inevitably start moving into the COO position. Combining a deep understanding of operations with the financial grounding that controllers live and breathe will become even more valuable as accountants from older generations retire or move out of the daily grind.

As we move into a more tech-focused future, your team will likely include not just accountants, but people who can fix that tech when things break. Jonathan sees a need for system administrators who understand what the system is doing, and can get in to fix things when your accounting sense tells you that something doesn't look right. You also may need to hire some developer types who can support the AI for a timely resolution "because support from software providers is usually not the fastest."

However, by 2050, you may be able to use whatever is the equivalent of ChatGPT to fix things that break. Enterprising developers today are using ChatGPT to write simple pieces of code.[6] Cloud software providers in 2050 may well include their own built-in bot that can diagnose and repair software on the fly.

The job of controller in the future won't go away, but Jerry thinks it may morph into more of a leader or quarterback who will be "ultimately held responsible for making sure that everything works and everything is flowing correctly." When systems can talk to each other and exchange data, "another ambitious goal is to have the least amount of people within finance as possible," says Jerry. The goal may be to "have one person that really is the quarterback to oversee what's going on." An extreme version of that vision is that maybe we'll have "no accounting department, but just systems communicating across the board and sharing information, then getting stuff done in an intelligent way," says Jerry. However, he still believes that having humans involved will be essential to ensure that outside parties, such as investors, government officials, auditors, and banks will have access to the information they need, but not full access to every part of your system.

THE GAP BETWEEN TECH ADOPTERS AND TECH LAGGARDS WILL GROW

What Mike sees as the biggest hindrance to technology advancement is actually adoption. Here at FloQast, we live in this bubble where everyone is on the cloud. But as FloQast moves upmarket and into new geographies, we're seeing that a large percentage of accountants are still living in the past.

They can't or won't look at the cloud. Some have huge bespoke systems that aren't easily automated. For many of these companies, Moore's Law is trumped by the inability to change security and compliance. These are very real challenges around adoption of new technology.

It's even worse when you look at the public sector. The IRS

makes headlines for using 50- and 60-year-old mainframe computers that run on COBOL.[7] Plenty of local and state governments still rely heavily on on-premise software and paper documents stored in massive file cabinets.

Cullen Zandstra, our CTO and co-founder, is a big AI thinker, and believes that technology will change the world. He's forever thinking about what more in accounting can be automated, and what that will mean for FloQast when the close and Ops are all fully automated. But even if everything was automated today, it will still be at least 10 or 15 years before everyone implements all the automations that cloud-native organizations take for granted today. Even if the technology that will work for a specific company exists today, there are still forces within accounting and within corporate governance that will delay a move to the cloud. Even just contemplating that move is a huge challenge for many organizations.

Companies like ours that got their start in the last decade or so, or that will be starting in the future, are almost universally choosing to build their systems from the ground up on cloud, AI and automation. Their accounting departments already look wildly different from that of a competitor founded 60 years ago. And this gap between cloud-native companies and those that haven't yet moved to the cloud will only get bigger.

So when you pick up your head in 2050, we predict that the split between tech adopters and tech laggards will be even more acute than what you see today. The level of tech deployed will depend heavily on the company culture and the mindset of the controller. If you have a controller who's basically accepted the level of manual work and isn't looking to automate anything, you're just going to be stuck in that cycle as long as that controller is there. Conversely, if you have a controller who's all about innovation, that department will look vastly different and will be way more effective.

Whether you're at a startup or at a company still using on-premise technology, adopting the Ops approach will be a requirement. If you're working in a startup, your operations are probably going to be pretty clean out of the gate as you start building everything from scratch, and you'll be well-suited to layer on technology and scale from there efficiently.

Our concern is for the companies that exist today and have poorly integrated or on-premises accounting infrastructure in place which means the team is just treading water. They will need to get the low-hanging fruit of Ops sorted out so they can compete with the new companies that started in the cloud. The first step is to get the processes sorted out so they understand what's going on. Then either purchase the appropriate technology or build the integrations needed to automate processes. Automation will buy the time they need to keep improving and keep getting better. These companies will have the biggest boosts from automation because there's just so much pain there as it is.

REPORTING WILL CHANGE

The basic model for financial reporting has been changing incrementally over time, as investors, decision-makers, and other stakeholders have been demanding more and more information. While the basic format of GAAP financials — the income statement, balance sheet, and statement of cash flows — haven't changed a whole lot in the last century, other reporting requirements continue to add more and more information to financials. Stefan foresees that as part of the expanding role of the accountant, "reporting will become more customized for the individual role." By 2050, "what we see today as being required will seem like a drop in the bucket," he says, and because the work is there, "we need to create the capacity to allow ourselves to get there."

The exponential expansions in computing power over the last few decades have accommodated this increase in reporting requirements. We don't see those rapid improvements in computing power for handling increasingly large data sets slowing down ever. Cloud technologies and other tech developments we can't even imagine today will allow accountants to build more intensive models that will provide us even more real-time insight into what's happening without the lag time or system slowdowns that prevent many ERPs from deploying tech that's available today. "But as computing power increases, we'll find ways to consume it," Stefan says. "We'll find ways to do new and more complex reporting very quickly, and the market will always find ways to use that data.

As we mentioned in Chapter 5, while GAAP is the universal standard for financial reporting, it doesn't always provide the information that the executive team or outside stakeholders need for making decisions. Internally, we use SaaS metrics, similar to the model described by Tien Tzuo in his book *Subscribed: Why the Subscription Model Will Be Your Company's Future — and What to Do About It.* But as of today, there aren't any standards around how SaaS metrics are calculated. This means that investors and analysts frequently have to deconstruct the metrics of SaaS companies to get to a true apples-to-apples comparison. We can see that in the next decade or so, as more and more parts of our economy move to subscription services, we will have international standards for SaaS reporting.

These days, you can't ignore the push for ESG reporting. Whether you think ESG reporting is a good thing or not, it's coming. It may seem like climate change is the political fuel pushing ESG reporting, but we see the push coming from investors and other stakeholders. And it won't be just climate change that companies will be reporting on. Investors will want to see if organizations really are doing work that supports their stated missions and goals, whether those goals have to do with climate change or diversity or community development. They want data to back up those assertions.

The push for ESG reporting today is something Stefan finds interesting because "it's one of the first signals from the marketplace that we will start using very different nontraditional data for reporting that we aren't now." This opens up what he considers a "zone of exploration, a new frontier of accounting." Including third-party data is something new for us, "and it's really hard to say where that will take us, but ESG is pointing us there."

Stefan believes that ERPs will be challenged to remain the center of enterprise tech, and that if the ERPs don't get behind ESG reporting, within 15 years, a whole new type of software will be developed that tracks that information in organizations. Over time, this new type of software will be at least equal in importance to our present-day ERPs. It may even overtake the role of ERPs for financial information within the organization.

As we've emphasized over and over in this book, the operational approach — and we would argue, the future of accounting itself — requires us to connect the dots between different parts of our organizations, and to get out of the silos of financial data and out into operations.

ESG reporting will force organizations to do just that because you need to connect to different types of data from different sources, validate it, and push it through to create reporting that's not just financial information. Some of it will be financial KPIs, but a lot of it will be OKRs or certain HR metrics or certain vendor information. It won't just be transactional data, but companies will have to consolidate it and report it. If the ERPs don't change the way their backends work and how their reporting works, a new company will come along and be the next Oracle.

Today, the investors and analysts are poring through information from all the sources available — investor calls, SEC filings, statements from leadership — and are struggling to interpret what it means. They're thinking "Can I trust what the CEO is saying? Can I trust the CFO or the chief sales officer or the other insiders?" Investors are having to buy what these people are saying without being able to see the inner workings of the company. They want to see more.

This is coming from activists and investors who are worried about climate change and social justice and diversity and inclusion. They care about how employees are treated, and they recognize that companies that pay attention to these things are more resilient and will continue to make good things that people want to buy. Over time, as these little political social fuels are consumed, this will change reporting completely.

Eventually, what will be left is linking company core values and mission to the financial performance of the company and to its valuation. Stefan believes this will cause a profound shift in company governance and will impact who will be the future CEOs and CFOs. It will be a lot easier to judge if the leaders have been effective when we have true reporting on what is actually happening within an organization. The people who are CEOs and CFOs today won't make it in the future. They're living their last golden years out.

HOW TO PREPARE FOR THIS FUTURE

A few years ago, futurists Peter Diamandis and Steven Kotler published their book, *The Future is Faster than You Think,* which discusses the ways that developments across many areas of technology are accelerating progress in other areas that are also accelerating. As one example, they point to the development of new drugs:

> *The speed of drug development is accelerating, not only because biotechnology is progressing at an exponential rate, but because artificial intelligence, quantum computing, and a couple other exponentials are converging on the field. In other words, these waves are starting to overlap, stacking atop one another, producing tsunami-sized behemoths that threaten to wash away most everything in their past.*

We see this synergistic acceleration among our most tech-savvy partners and customers. As cloud ERPs get better, there are more and more tech tools available to automate specific parts of workflows. These automations make it easier for the businesses of our customers to create more advanced products and services, which in turn require more advanced tech for their accounting and planning functions. And as ERPs belatedly improve their own internal reconciliation and month-end close processes, we at FloQast are driven to keep making our new products better and even more ridiculously simple to implement and use.

We don't know what will be coming along, but as Jerry Raphael says, the best way to prepare "is to roll with an open mind. And continue to keep learning, and improving your skills." The skills you'll need in the future won't be the same as what you need to be able to do today. "Tasks go away, and there are things we used to do that we don't have to do anymore," says Razzak. The first calculators replaced pen and paper calculations, and spreadsheets in turn replaced calculators, and software is replacing the modeling and planning that used to be done with spreadsheets. "And now just about everything is digital," Razzak continues. "So a controller or a CFO in 2050 will have more technology and ability to process data and pull out insights than ever before."

Just imagine: The majority of the tasks that people do on a day-to-day basis to keep operations moving forward will change drastically. The skills you have today may well be obsolete, just as you no longer need to be good with a 10-key to be an accountant. But what won't change is the central role of accounting and data to the success of a business.

We have no idea what the next big development in accounting tech will be. No one does. Accounting technology is sure to evolve in the next few decades in ways that we can't imagine. But the continuous thread from the paper ledgers of the past to the cloud ERPs of the present has been the accountant's discipline around getting the numbers right, the need for consistent processes, and the constant push for efficiency. These won't change, no matter how much the tech changes. Even if tech evolves to the complete automation envisioned by Jerry Raphael, where systems talk to each other with little human intervention, there will still be the need for accountants who can make sure that the executives get the information they need when they need it, and that they can trust it.

Here at FloQast, while we are leveraging AI and all the tech that comes our way with attention first and foremost on data security, our approach has always been to support accountants in working the way that they work, by providing visibility and accountability in process workflows.

What we do know is that if you start implementing the Ops approach now, and learn as much as you can about how the other parts of your organization work, you'll be better positioned to take advantage of whatever comes your way. The ability to communicate effectively with a wide variety of people and to understand their perspective on what's important to their jobs will always serve you well. Combine that communication and understanding with the discipline of being an accountant and our innate ability to solve puzzles and make things better and you will have no problems with whatever comes along in 2050.

13 / THE GRAND VISION

Past vs Future

Tactical operative of the past	to	Strategic leader of the future
Number cruncher	▶	Operational leader
Spreadsheet wrangler	▶	Performance driver
Number tie-out specialist	▶	Data/business storyteller
Bogged down & burned out	▶	Elevated and empowered

Even over our careers as millennial accountants, we've seen a shift in the work responsibilities of controllers and CFOs from mainly closing the books to taking on more of a strategic role. A shift from being the Office of No to taking the lead on digital transformation. And we're thrilled to see a growing number of controllers around the world who are diving into Ops and applying the discipline of accounting to make their organizations better. These shifts, from purely tactical number crunchers to strategic leaders in the future are in the figure above.

The pandemic accelerated the shift from a purely tactical role to a strategic role. Ongoing talent pipeline pressures at the same time that boomers are leaving — or have left — combined with 3 million to 5 million new businesses starting every year,[1] mean that accounting departments will have to be even more creative in finding ways to do more with fewer people.

BY 2050, MOST COOS WILL HAVE COME UP THROUGH ACCOUNTING

This is our grand vision. Within just 26 years, accounting will be the center of the organization, and most COOs will move up from accounting.

This will be a change from the way it historically has been, as this 2006 article from the Harvard Business Review[2] explains:

> *When you start to examine COOs as a class, one thing immediately becomes clear: There are almost no constants. People with very different backgrounds ascend to the role and succeed in it. This variability makes the job difficult to study; it's hard to know whether you are making proper inferences when comparing one COO with another.*

While we can't absolutely predict what the career path in 2050 will look like, we can say that adopting the Ops mindset and approach will open far more doors than it will close, and that some of those opened doors will lead to the COO seat. "Once you start getting out into the business, you gain all this other experience," explains Greg Vecellio, our controller at FloQast. "And that sets you up to say, 'I am more than just an accountant. I don't have to be a controller or a CFO or a CAO.

I can be a COO.'" Controllers who expand into Ops will have "the best of both worlds," Greg continues. "You understand the Ops, but you also have the financial grounding, which a lot of people don't have."

The world is your oyster.

By implementing the ideas in this book, you'll be well on your way to qualifying for the COO role. Mastering the skills and building the knowledge base of how operations work takes time. This isn't an instant fix for a dysfunctional and chaotic organization. But by moving ahead, one step, one process, and one area at a time, you can make things better over time. The reward is work that's more fun, and making the 40-hour work-week the norm — not the exception.

You're going to enjoy this version of accounting a lot more than today's version.

HOW ACCOUNTANTS TAKE OVER BUSINESS

We've already laid out in detail the process for moving into an Ops approach in Chapter 9, but here's a quick recap.

First, **start with the close**. The close is a highly iterative process and it's what you know. It happens every month, every quarter, every year, so this is the easiest place to start learning the process of operationalizing. In many organizations, there's lots of low-hanging fruit here, so you can get some easy wins and create operational capacity for bigger projects. You'll have better luck if you put your workflows in a central platform to document, automate, track, and optimize the processes in your playbook, as we discussed in Chapter 10.

Next, **expand across the office of the CFO.** Getting your own house in order is a must before you start trying to fix organization-wide operations. As controller, you'll find yourself overseeing a bit of finance and reporting and a bit of tax in all your workflows, and you have broad insight into all of the operations of finance, so you are positioned perfectly to optimize and streamline all those workflows. This also will help expand your skills in leadership so you're not seen as the one who says "No," but the one who works to make things better.

Keep in mind that fixing things internally will sometimes require you to address external functional issues, and then come back to the internal workflows. For example, if there's a problem with inventory, you won't be able to cut days off the close until you figure out what the hangup with inventory is.

By fixing that upstream problem and making that process better, the close also improves. This is where you start to build credibility and leadership with the organization, which you can use as a springboard for future collaboration. People will start to see accounting not as the Office of No, as obstructionist bean counters, but as a valuable resource for making things better.

Once the finance and accounting functions are under control, **begin to fold in other functions' recurring workflows.** To some extent, every job is at least somewhat iterative, even if people don't think it is. The most mundane and repetitive roles are generally the lower, entry-level positions. Try to help these contributors first, so instead of trying to help the inventory manager, see if you can help the inventory specialist. Besides helping improve some of the most painful jobs in the organization, you'll gain insights to help their managers and directors. And often, fixing the bottlenecks at the bottom has huge cascading impacts throughout the organization.

Slowly add more and more functions. Keep adding more functions and ask people across the organization about their processes and what's working, what's not working, and where the bottlenecks are. As more parts of the company start seeing the benefits of evening out the workload and automating manual processes, you'll have an easier time adding more functions and recurring processes.

As you're working on optimizing workflows across the organization, don't forget that this is only part of your job. You can't neglect your other deliverables: the reporting, the KPIs, and the storytelling around the deliverables. Improving workflows will make providing those deliverables easier. You'll also have the capacity and the depth of perception so that those deliverables provide the additional levels of detail and insight that leadership of a growing organization requires.

Identify wasted time and improve that area. This is the never-ending piece of the job. How do we make our business more and more efficient every month? But the benefit is that everyone's job will ultimately keep getting better. A few years later, pick up your head and see that the entire company is being orchestrated by accounting. This is the way to get to do more fulfilling work.

THE PATH FORWARD FOR ACCOUNTING

While improving Ops is important and too often overlooked, it's not a silver bullet for ensuring your organization achieves its strategic goals. Improving Ops is more of a catalyst to enable those strategic objectives. It creates the company-wide bandwidth that allows everyone to work as an army marching in synchrony toward a goal.

This grand vision of COOs coming up through accounting won't happen without some effort on the part of controllers. "The more a controller is open to embracing new tools and technologies, the more likely that is to happen," says Razzak. New tools and new technologies will replace the tools and technologies we use today so that we have more ability to pull insights out of the data. "But it's going to be a lot more about understanding the core concepts of the business, and how they interact with each other, and being able to use that technology either to make things more efficient, or to gain the cross-functional insights needed to make better decisions and drive things forward," Razzak continues. "Accounting is at that nexus of data between what's already happened and what's happening going forward," which puts controllers in a good position to make this grand vision a reality.

This grand vision isn't just about extending the purview of accountants beyond the office of the CFO, but about creating a culture and processes for making the entire organization better. The ultimate goal is to provide company leaders with better data on a more timely basis so that the insights about the past are deeper and the decisions for the future are better.

We believe this is the path forward for accounting. Accountants already have a unique skill set around process improvement. Adopting the Ops approach creates the muscle of constant improvement through measured and iterative processes.

The companies with the COOs who rise up through the ranks as operational accountants will be the ones where everything is smoother and faster. They'll be the companies agile enough to ride the waves of disruption as massive as the COVID-19 pandemic and come out unscathed. They'll be the companies so firmly in touch with the market that their latest products and services constantly delight and amaze their customers. And they'll be the ones that endure well into this next century.

Now go out and make it happen!

APPENDIX

1 / *PRODUCT AND MARKETING WORKFLOWS*

Management guru Peter Drucker famously said "The purpose of a business is to create and keep a customer." The way that businesses do that is by creating products or services that either fix a pain point or embody something that people didn't know they wanted or needed until they see it. Smart phones are a prime example of the latter. Tech companies like FloQast do both. That's the product part. Marketing is the part of a company that spreads the word about what the company sells.

The challenge for controllers moving into Ops is that most of us know very little about either product or marketing. It's not generally taught in our accounting courses, except as expenditures that either get capitalized as cost of goods sold or expensed as SG&A. The work of these two areas looks a lot different from closing the books every month and getting quarterly financials out.

Because both of us are accountants first, we're deferring to our former Director of Product Marketing, Colleen Wanty, to explain how this works together.

THE PRAGMATIC INSTITUTE FRAMEWORK FOR GO-TO-MARKET STRATEGY

By Colleen Wanty

Product Marketing is a connector that sits between Product — the ones who create the solutions and features a company sells — and Marketing — the ones who communicate with the market about those products. Product Marketing helps create a positioning framework for the product to drive an emotional connection with the value proposition of the product. This also includes looking at a variety of factors like the competitive set and macro marketing factors that influence how you speak to these features. Product Marketing also translates what the product does and what problems it solves into the language used by buyers so they have an emotional connection with the value proposition. There are times when a product offer may need to be rebundled or restructured so it meshes with pain points of the buyers. The goal of product marketing is to bring solutions to market with targeted messaging for the buyers and influencers, a concise story of value with supporting data, and proof points of that value.

BUILDING A BETTER MOUSETRAP ISN'T ENOUGH

A crucial function of every company is introducing that better mousetrap to the world so that the people who would buy a better mousetrap learn about it. Companies that have that better mousetrap fail all the time if they don't know how to introduce that new product to the market. They also fail when there's a lack of internal alignment about what that new product is going to be, or even what to call it when they're talking to customers or even to each other.

Here at FloQast, we've been following the rough framework from the Pragmatic Institute for our go-to-market or GTM strategy that you see below.[1] In general, the top part is the responsibility of Product Marketing and the bottom is the responsibility of the Product team, but often some of the boxes are exchanged. Optimally, these two parts of the organization work very closely together.

<table>
<tr><td></td><td></td><td>Business Plan</td><td>Positioning</td><td>Market Plan</td><td></td><td></td></tr>
<tr><td>Market Problems</td><td>Market Definition</td><td>Pricing</td><td>Buyer Experience</td><td>Revenue Growth</td><td></td><td></td></tr>
<tr><td>Win/Loss Analysis</td><td>Distribution Strategy</td><td>Buy, Build or Partner</td><td>Buyer Personas</td><td>Revenue Retention</td><td></td><td></td></tr>
<tr><td>Distinctive Competencies</td><td>Product Portfolio</td><td>Product Profitability</td><td>User Personas</td><td>Launch</td><td></td><td></td></tr>
<tr><th>MARKET</th><th>FOCUS</th><th>BUSINESS</th><th>PLANNING</th><th>PROGRAMS</th><th>ENABLEMENT</th><th>SUPPORT</th></tr>
<tr><td>Competitive Landscape</td><td>Product Roadmap</td><td>Innovation</td><td>Requirements</td><td>Awareness</td><td>Sales Alignment</td><td>Programs</td></tr>
<tr><td>Asset Assessment</td><td></td><td></td><td>Use Scenarios</td><td>Nurturing</td><td>Content</td><td>Operations</td></tr>
<tr><td></td><td></td><td></td><td>Stakeholder Communications</td><td>Advocacy</td><td>Sales Tools</td><td>Events</td></tr>
<tr><td></td><td></td><td></td><td></td><td>Measurement</td><td>Channel Training</td><td>Channels</td></tr>
</table>

STRATEGY

EXECUTION

From https://www.pragmaticinstitute.com/framework/

When we started using this framework from the Pragmatic Institute, it helped us assess our product and marketing operations to find the holes and ensure that our activities were all aligned. We used it to develop our playbook for each iteration of the GTM cycle. That helped us match the activities that had to happen with the process of moving from a vision of the next product to developing that product and getting it out into the market and into the hands of our customers. Our operations around product marketing are more efficient because we're all working from the same playbook. While the GTM cycle always tends to be more controlled chaos than disciplined action, this framework gives us a way to make things a little better each time.

MARKET

It all starts with the visionaries who make the decisions about the products that will move from upper left to right, from strategy to execution. Our visionaries at FloQast are Mike, Chris Sluty and Cullen Zandstra. This works really well for early stage organizations, and even as the company grows. It is also important to have a well-defined feedback loop from customers as that is also a datapoint for innovation. Another input to this process is to keep an eye on current and emerging competitors. And lastly, when you can afford it, it's worthwhile to engage industry analysts because they can talk to even more companies that you may not be engaged with as you enter new markets.

For the customers, this next iteration should make sense that your company would be the ones to solve the problem, and that they trust you to solve that problem. It is important to think of your market as a bullseye: it is important to not innovate so far away from the center that you cannot be credible with an innovation.

One of the things that has held us in good stead is that Mike and Chris are not software developers, but were users who built software. As a result, the product was intuitive because they wanted it to be intuitive to them.

FOCUS

Any new product or improvement to an existing product should be something that your organization has the capability of making and getting out to the market without blowing up other parts of your organization. It helps if it fits into your existing distribution strategy, so that you have a sales team who already knows the target market. It should also fit in with the product portfolio and the product roadmap.

BUSINESS

Next comes the business plan. This is where you start thinking about pricing, and whether you want to buy, build or partner with someone to make it. The business plan needs to address essential questions like the following:

- How many of these will we sell?
- What will it cost to build it?
- Will this be profitable?

Many companies don't bring Marketing in until this stage, but to be really effective, you need to engage marketing from the very beginning.

PLANNING

Once you've established what the product will be, who the market is, and why it makes sense, Marketing starts working on positioning. About this time, Product goes off and starts to build the product. When they get a minimum viable product, they start the beta process. From those first few beta customers, Marketing learns a lot about the product, and starts to develop buyer personas and user personas, based on who in a company is the buyer and who are the users.

Sometimes the buyer is not who you expect it to be. We thought most of the users and buyers for one of our new products would be the controller, but it turned out that the internal auditors were the ones most excited about it. From the beta process, Product also learns about user requirements and how this tech will be used within companies. All of this data will ultimately become part of the marketing plan at launch.

Some of what you learn in the beta process will shape both the product and the language you use to explain what the new product does. When we started working on our Reconciliation Management product, we saw that the competition was saying that they would automate all the reconciliations. But when we talked to the accountants, they told us that there would be some accounts that they would never want to automate. These accounts might have a low transaction volume, but high risk. Or they're equity accounts. Or the balances might be material, or require some judgment. So the language we went to market with was "All Recs are not equal." Some won't be automated, and some belong in a spreadsheet. But you can manage all of those and have a full view of all of your recs.

Naming the product is a crucial and overlooked step. Here at FloQast, we work with accountants, who tend to think in concrete terms, so we have followed a line of naming our products pretty much what they do. The name identifies the pain point it solves. This contrasts with companies that make direct-to-consumer products like fashion or cosmetics, where abstract names are more effective because it often involves one product or related product lines.

This name also needs to be what everyone in the company calls the new product. You can't have sales team members calling it A and the customer success team calling it B. Your customers will get confused when customer success tries to help them optimize B, and the customers have no idea what B is because they know it as A.

Another aspect of the product and marketing is that people overlook is the synergy between color, design and words. When I started marketing, people would just pick a color. But when you see how well it comes together with people who are really gifted with color and words, you can see the impact. Apple definitely understands this, and you can see it in the design of their products and their ads and even how the stores look.

PROGRAMS

With any new product, you don't want to lose a prospect or customer to a competitor when you have a minimum viable product because they don't know about your new offer. The revenue retention part of the marketing plan means you go into the existing customer base and tell them about the new product as soon as possible. The minute the customer starts to look elsewhere, you're in a battle to retain that customer. The marketing plan also includes the methods for building awareness, nurturing leads and determining how you will measure success.

ENABLEMENT AND SUPPORT

Next, you need to get the company, and especially sales, aligned around this new product. That means educating sales about the new product and creating sales enablement tools they can use to quickly explain the new product to prospects. This is an iterative and continuous process that takes more than one meeting to get everyone on board.

Customer success also needs to understand every new product so that if a customer calls and asks for an install, they are ready to respond.

CONSIDER YOUR CUSTOMER'S CALENDAR WHEN YOU DEVELOP YOUR OWN

As part of launch planning, we look at our customers' calendar of events throughout the year. Accountants have a very stringent regulatory calendar that impacts the timing of when we release new products. For example, January is always a bad month. It's hard to get their attention, so Product Marketing at FloQast sometimes has to push back on the dev team to wait a month or two to release something big.

Other times we'll look ahead and wait to launch a product so that it comes out when the problem it solves is top of mind. For example, when we have products that help with the documentation needed for audits, we plan the release of those for May. It's right after the audit, and companies that come out of the audit with control findings will be motivated to find a solution that fixes the problems for next year.

We do this full exercise for new product launches or launches of major features. Tech companies are constantly putting out enhancements. Those smaller updates or bug fixes require fewer steps. Depending on how big the product is, you may be working on this over several quarters, and you may have multiple things going on at the same time.

THE HARDEST PARTS OF PRODUCT MARKETING

Evolutionarily, we're hardwired to understand pictures. Ancient peoples understood "two rivers and a mountain" long before we had the written word. A good starting point in marketing is to try to tell the story with a really good picture. A flowchart or a graphic can be much more effective than a 45-page document with detailed instructions. But telling a story with pictures and just a few words is hard to do.

It's even harder to tell a story in just a few words. Most people outside of marketing just see that final five-word phrase that encapsulates the full message, and they don't see the 600 words that it takes to get to those final five amazing words that capture the whole message.

Another challenge is that product marketers don't always directly manage the people we're working with. Every launch requires a cross-functional matrix group with people from Product Management, Sales, Customer Success, and Marketing. Most of these people don't report to anyone in Product Marketing. While everyone ultimately reports to the CEO, it's not a good use of that person's time to drive a launch. It can be like herding cats to get people across the company moving in the same direction to launch something new. Getting all the pieces aligned and keeping everyone working together as a coordinated group usually takes the force of personality.

2 / *RESOURCES*

RECOMMENDED PODCASTS

1. Blood Sweat and Balance Sheets
2. The FinTech Flo Podcast
3. The Fraud Files
4. Accounting Podcast
5. Accounting Today Podcast
6. CFO Thought Leader Podcast
7. The Soul of Enterprise

BOOKS

1. *Controllers Code: The Secret Formula for a Successful Career in Finance* by Michael Whitmire
2. *The Future of the Professions: How Technology Will Transform the Work of Human Experts* by Richard Susskind and Daniel Susskind
3. *Thank You for Arguing: What Aristotle, Lincoln, and Homer Simpson Can Teach Us About the Power of Persuasion* by Jay Heinrichs

4. *Who: The A Method for Hiring* by Geoff Smart and Randy Street
5. *Organizational Awareness: A Primer* by George Pitagorsky, Daniel Goleman, Richard Boyatzkis, Vanessa Druskat, and Michele Nevarez
6. *The Future is Faster than You Think: How Converging Technologies Are Transforming Business, Industries, and Our Lives* by Peter H. Diamandis and Steven Kotler
7. *Subscribed: Why the Subscription Model Will Be Your Company's Future — and What to Do About It* by Tien Tzuo

OTHER

Toastmasters

NOTES

INTRODUCTION: OPERATIONAL ACCOUNTING IN REAL LIFE

1. Andreas Behrendt, Axel Karlsson, Tarek Kasah, and Daniel Swan, "The CEO: Architect of the new operations agenda," McKinsey: Operations, December 6, 2021. https://www.mckinsey.com/business-functions/operations/our-insights/the-ceo-architect-of-the-new-operations-agenda

2. THE PRESSURE COOKER OF ACCOUNTING TODAY

1. "Controller's Guidebook: When Accountants Dare to Dream," FloQast, July 2023, https://floqast.com/controllers-guidebook/dare-to-dream/.
2. "Understanding Small Business in America," 2016, U.S. Chamber of Commerce Foundation, https://www.uschamberfoundation.org/smallbizregs/.
3. Clyde Wayne Crews, "Ten Thousand Commandments 2022: An Annual Snapshot of the Federal Regulatory State, Competitive Enterprise Institute, 2022, https://cei.org/studies/ten-thousand-commandments-2022/.
4. "Time spent per week by compliance teams updating policies and procedures in order to reflect the latest regulations worldwide from 2011 to 2020," Statista, https://www.statista.com/statistics/656873/time-spent-per-week-by-compliance-teams-updating-procedures/#:~:text=This%20statistic%20shows%20the%20comparison,reflect%20the%20current%20regulatory%20rules.
5. "Tracking the Cost of Complying with Government Regulation," National Bureau of Economic Research, February 2023, https://www.nber.org/digest/20232/tracking-cost-complying-government-regulation#:~:text=The%20average%20US%20firm%20spends,(NBER%20Working%20Paper%2030691).
6. VIX Volatility Index – Historical Chart, https://www.macrotrends.net/2603/vix-volatility-index-historical-chart.
7. Anita Dennis, "A Good Hire is Hard to Find," Journal of Accountancy, September 30, 1998, https://www.journalofaccountancy.com/issues/1998/oct/dennisb.html.
8. Alexandra L. Gabbin, "Warning Signs about the Future Supply of Accounting Graduates," CPA Journal, September 2019, https://www.

cpajournal.com/2019/10/11/warning-signs-about-the-future-supply-of-accounting-graduates/.

9. "2021 Trends: A report on accounting education, the CPA Exam and public accounting firms' hiring of recent graduates," AICPA, 2022, https://www.aicpa.org/professional-insights/download/2021-trends-report.
10. "2023 Trends: A report on accounting education, the CPA Exam, and public accounting firms' hiring of recent graduates," AICPA, 2023, https://www.aicpa-cima.com/professional-insights/download/2023-trends-report.
11. "A CPA Pipeline Report: Decoding the Decline," Illinois Society of CPAs, 2021, https://www.icpas.org/information/professional-issues/decoding-the-decline
12. "New Startups Break Record in 2021: Unpacking the Numbers", Economic Innovation Group, January 19, 2021, https://eig.org/new-start-ups-break-record-in-2021-unpacking-the-numbers/
13. "Business Formation Statistics," United States Census Bureau, January 11, 2024, https://www.census.gov/econ/bfs/current/index.html.
14. "Gartner says Finance Departments With Differentiated Cultures Can Reduce Hiring Compensation Premiums by 50%," Gartner Newsroom, August 7, 2019, https://www.gartner.com/en/newsroom/press-releases/2019-08-07-gartner-says-finance-departments-with-differentiated-.
15. "Exposure Draft: Proposed Revisions to AICPA/NASBA Uniform Accountancy Act and NASBA Uniform Accountancy Act Rules, Section 6(d) and Rule 6-7," AICPA.org, November 2015, https://us.aicpa.org/content/dam/aicpa/advocacy/state/downloadabledocuments/inactive-retired-exposure-draft-nov-2015.pdf.
16. Benjamin Romberg, "Finance Exodus: How the great resignation is coming for finance teams," Spendesk (blog), December 13,2021, https://blog.spendesk.com/en/finance-exodus-great-resignation.
17. "PwC Pulse Survey: Next in Work," PwC Research and Insights, 2021, https://www.pwc.com/us/en/library/pulse-survey/future-of-work.html.
18. Lindsey Ellis, "Why So Many Accountants Are Quitting," Wall Street Journal, December 28, 2022, https://www.wsj.com/articles/why-so-many-accountants-are-quitting-11672236016?mod=article_inline.
19. Mark Maurer, "Job Security Isn't Enough to Keep Many Accountants from Quitting," Wall Street Journal, September 22, 2023, https://www.wsj.com/articles/accounting-quit-job-security-675fc28f.
20. "Controller's Guidebook: The Great Recalibration: The Role of Technology in Retaining and Recruiting Accountants," FloQast, March 2023, https://floqast.com/controllers-guidebook/the-great-recalibration/.
21. "Controller's Guidebook: Burnout in Accounting: Understanding the

Problem, Leveraging Solutions," FloQast, July 2022, https://floqast.com/controllers-guidebook/burnout-in-accounting/.

22. "PwC Pulse Survey: Next in Work," PwC Research and Insights, 2021, https://www.pwc.com/us/en/library/pulse-survey/future-of-work.html.
23. "The Smart Financial Close: Market Research from Dynamic Insights," Ventana Research and FloQast, 2023, https://www.ventanaresearch.com/dynamic_insight/office_of_finance/research_report/2022 .
24. "The Digital Controller/CFO: Benchmark Study 2021," Controllers Council, 2021, https://controllerscouncil.org/resources/digital-controller-cfo-study-report-2021/.
25. Mark Maurer, "Why You Don't Need to Be an Accountant to Be a CFO," The Wall Street Journal, January 29, 2020, https://www.wsj.com/articles/companies-appointing-fewer-finance-chiefs-with-accounting-skills-11580293801
26. Jennifer Wilson-Alvarez, "Companies Broaden CFO's Responsibilities to Retain Them in Strong Job Market," Wall Street Journal, July 4, 2022, https://www.wsj.com/articles/companies-broaden-cfos-responsibilities-to-retain-them-in-strong-job-market-11656936002?reflink=desktopwebshare_permalink.

3. WHAT IS OPERATIONAL ACCOUNTING?

1. David Sacks, "The Cadence: How to Operate a SaaS Startup," Medium, Craft Ventures (blog), July 1, 2020, https://medium.com/craft-ventures/the-cadence-how-to-operate-a-saas-startup-436aa8099e8

5. WHY ACCOUNTING SHOULD TAKE OVER OPERATIONS

1. "Killing Strategy: The Disruption of Management Consulting," Research Briefs. CB Insights, October 8, 2020, https://www.cbinsights.com/research/disrupting-management-consulting/.
2. Lauren Thomas, "Peloton hires McKinsey to review cost structure as equipment sales slow," CNBC, January 18, 2022, https://www.cnbc.com/2022/01/18/peloton-hires-mckinsey-to-review-cost-structure-as-equipment-sales-slow-.html.
3. "Adapting to Endure," Sequoia Capital, All-Hands Slide Deck, May 2022, https://content.fortune.com/wp-content/uploads/2022/05/Adapting_to_Endure_May_2022.pdf.

6. ADVANTAGES OF MOVING INTO AN OPERATIONAL APPROACH

1. "Controller's Guidebook: The Great Recalibration: The Role of Technology in Retaining and Recruiting Accountants," FloQast, March 2023, https://floqast.com/controllers-guidebook/the-great-recalibration/.
2. "Controller's Guidebook: When Accountants Dare to Dream," FloQast, July 2023, https://floqast.com/controllers-guidebook/dare-to-dream/.

7. HOW THE OPS APPROACH SOLVES THE TWO BIGGEST ISSUES OF EVERY BUSINESS

1. "The State of Business Communication," Grammarly, 2022, https://www.grammarly.com/business/Grammarly_The_State_Of_Business_Communication.pdf.
2. Chelsea R. Lide and Francis J. Flynn, "Communication Miscalibration: The Price Leaders Pay for Not Sharing Enough," *Academy of Management Journal.* Vol. 66, Issue 4, Pages 1102-1122, August 2023, https://www.gsb.stanford.edu/faculty-research/publications/communication-miscalibration-price-leaders-pay-not-sharing-enough.
3. "The great attrition stems from a great disconnect," McKinsey & Company, October 18, 2021, https://www.mckinsey.com/featured-insights/sustainable-inclusive-growth/chart-of-the-day/the-great-attrition-stems-from-a-great-disconnect.
4. Ben Wigert and Sangeeta Agrawal, "Employee Burnout, Part 1: The 5 Main Causes," Gallup Workplace, July 12, 2018, https://www.gallup.com/workplace/237059/employee-burnout-part-main-causes.aspx.
5. Daniel Goleman, "A Sixth Sense for Reading Your Company," Korn Ferry Leadership, 2017, https://www.kornferry.com/insights/this-week-in-leadership/organizational-awareness-leadership.

8. WHAT SKILLS DO ACCOUNTANTS NEED TO DEVELOP FOR THE OPERATIONAL ROLE?

1. "The Controller's Guidebook: Through the Eye of the Storm and Closing Faster than Before," FloQast, 2021, https://get.floqast.com/2021-controllers-guidebook-through-the-eye-of-the-storm/.
2. "The Controller's Guidebook: Is Your Relationship with Technology a Solution to Burnout or a Source of Stress?" FloQast, May 2023, https://floqast.com/controllers-guidebook/relationship-with-accounting-technology/.
3. "The Smart Financial Close: Market Insight from Dynamic Insights,"

Ventana Research in partnership https://www.ventanaresearch.com/dynamic_insight/office_of_finance/research_report/2022 .

9. HOW DO YOU MOVE INTO AN OPERATIONAL ROLE?

1. James Kosur, "GE runs an intense 5-year program to develop executives, and only 2% finish it," Business Insider, October 5, 2015, https://www.businessinsider.com/ge-green-beret-executive-development-program.
2. Nina Trentmann and Ted Mann, "GE Disbands Corporate Audit Program," Wall Street Journal, November 11, 2020, https://www.wsj.com/articles/ge-disbands-corporate-audit-program-11605090602#.
3. "Great Expectations: Making Hybrid Work Work," Work Trend Index Annual Report, Microsoft, March 16, 2022, https://www.microsoft.com/en-us/worklab/work-trend-index/great-expectations-making-hybrid-work-work.
4. Jane Thier, "Microsoft's remote-work-friendly CEO puts his finger on the big problem with working from home," Fortune, October 17, 2022, https://fortune.com/2022/10/17/microsoft-ceo-satya-nadella-remote-work-problem-productivity-paranoia/.

10. CREATING YOUR WORKFLOW PLAYBOOK

1. "The Controller's Guidebook: Is Your Relationship with Technology a Solution to Burnout or a Source of Stress?" FloQast, May 2023, https://floqast.com/controllers-guidebook/relationship-with-accounting-technology/.
2. "The Controller's Guidebook: Is Your Relationship with Technology a Solution to Burnout or a Source of Stress?" FloQast, May 2023, https://floqast.com/controllers-guidebook/relationship-with-accounting-technology/.

11. ESTABLISHING A CADENCE TO YOUR WORKFLOW

1. David Sacks, "The Cadence: How to Operate a SaaS Startup," Medium, Craft Ventures (blog), July 1, 2020, https://medium.com/craft-ventures/the-cadence-how-to-operate-a-saas-startup-436aa8099e8.

12. WHAT WILL ACCOUNTING LOOK LIKE IN 2050?

1. Jim McGregor and Tirias Research, "The True Nature Of Moore's Law – Driving Innovation For The Next 50 Years," Forbes, October 7, 2022, https://www.forbes.com/sites/tiriasresearch/2022/10/07/the-true-

nature-of-moores-law--driving-innovation-for-the-next-50-years/?sh=679e37271aa3.

2. Kif Lefswing, "Intel says Moore's Law is still alive and well. Invidia says it's ended," CNBC, September 27, 2022, https://www.cnbc.com/2022/09/27/intel-says-moores-law-is-still-alive-nvidia-says-its-ended.html.
3. Thomas Frey, "The Great AI Disruption: Six Startling Predictions That Will Shape Our Lives and Test Our Limits," Foresight Journaling (blog), Futurist Speaker, May 4, 2023, https://futuristspeaker.com/artificial-intelligence/the-great-ai-disruption-six-startling-predictions-that-will-shape-our-lives-and-test-our-limits/.
4. Thomas Frey, "Unleashing the Future: Extreme Scenarios of How Smart Contracts Will Alter the Course of History," Foresight Journaling (blog), Futurist Speaker, June 1, 2023, https://futuristspeaker.com/future-scenarios/unleashing-the-future-extreme-scenarios-of-how-smart-contracts-will-alter-the-course-of-history/.
5. Jennifer Korn, "50 years ago, he made the first cell phone call," CNN Business, April 3, 2023, https://www.cnn.com/2023/04/03/tech/cell-phone-turns-50/index.html.
6. David Gewirtz, "How to use ChatGPT to write code," ZDNet, February 22. 2024, https://www.zdnet.com/article/how-to-use-chatgpt-to-write-code/.
7. "Outdated and Old IT Systems Slow Government and Put Taxpayers at Risk," Watchblog: Following the Federal Dollar, U.S. Government Accountability Office, February 14, 2023, https://www.gao.gov/blog/outdated-and-old-it-systems-slow-government-and-put-taxpayers-risk.

13. THE GRAND VISION

1. "How Many New Businesses Are Started Each Year? New Data Reveals the Answer," Commerce Institute, January 2024, https://www.commerceinstitute.com/new-businesses-started-every-year/.
2. Nate Bennett and Stephen A. Miles, "Second in Command: The Misunderstood Role of the Chief Operating Officer," Harvard Business Review (Magazine), May 2006, https://hbr.org/2006/05/second-in-command-the-misunderstood-role-of-the-chief-operating-officer.

1. PRODUCT AND MARKETING WORKFLOWS

1. "The Perfect Solution to Product: The Pragmatic Framework," Pragmatic Institute, https://www.pragmaticinstitute.com/framework/.

ACKNOWLEDGMENTS

Mike Whitmire

When we released "Controller's Code: The Secret Formula to a Successful Career in Finance" in April 2020, it felt like exactly what it was: the culmination of a pretty major undertaking. This was a project that grew into something a lot more challenging than what I had in mind when I thought out loud, "I should write a book."

I don't remember if the timing was strategic or not — considering the events of the world in the months immediately preceding the book launch — but the end result was exactly what we had hoped for: A reevaluation of the role of the controller and its place in a business. It touched on leadership, skills and experiences that effective managers possess, and the role that technology plays in dictating what accounting teams can and can't do.

When it was done, there was a collective exhale. We were incredibly proud of the end result, but also very, very ready to get back to work.

Well, here we are again, 4+ years and a lot of world events later, and *Code* still feels like the right stepping stone to get to the book you're reading now.

My co-author, FloQast Accounting Operational Evangelist Stefan van Duyvendijk, is one of the savvier accounting minds

I've ever met. Working with him and Liz on this project felt so organic — like an ongoing conversation — and was an absolute pleasure.

We wouldn't be anywhere without my co-founders, Cullen Zandstra and Chris Sluty. Over the years, I've realized how much I appreciate them just being there — their perspective, their experiences, their concerns, and our collective ability to complement each other with our different approaches to, well, everything.

Liz Farr once again helped harness our thoughts and experiences into a clear narrative, utilizing her unique blend of accounting experience with her innate ability to craft a story.

Just as it was four years ago, this project required a ton of time and collaboration. This book wouldn't exist without Kyle Cabodi, FloQast's Director of Corporate Communications. Kyle took this project not long after he joined the company and ran with it, keeping things moving when it seemed like there wasn't any time for anyone to be focusing on it.

Finally, I'd like to thank my family: Mom, Alison, and Harper — my world. I hope you realize how much you mean to me and how much you inspire me.

Go Dodgers.

Stefan van Duyvendijk

I would like to extend my heartfelt thanks to everyone who takes the time to read this book and reflect on its content. Finding the time and motivation to focus on professional growth can be challenging in our busy lives. I hope this book helps you on your journey.

A special thank you goes to Liz Farr, whose tireless efforts were instrumental in helping me put pen to paper. Liz, your dedication to this project, insightful contributions, and endless work hours made this book possible.

I also want to deeply thank Kyle Cabodi for his unwavering patience and dedication. Kyle, you kept the engine running smoothly and kept me on track. This project would not have been possible without your support.

Thank you to all the contributors who shared their real stories. I believe the best learning comes from shared experiences, and your willingness to share yours has enriched this book immensely.

A huge thank you to Mike Whitmire for including me in his grand vision for the future of accounting. Knowing that others share my passion and perspective on the industry has been incredibly validating.

I also want to acknowledge a few of my former bosses and professors who played a significant role in my growth as an accountant and professional: John Lietchy, Robert Peay, Ed Brice, Jerry Van Os, Richard Henage, Jennifer Harrison, Alan Rogers, Carmen Kaminski, and Nancy Panos Schmitt. Your guidance and mentorship have been invaluable.

To my accounting mentors and friends—Josh Gertsch, Joe Strain, Eric Plackett, Stefanie Foster, and Scott Olson—thank you for your support and for helping me grow more than anyone else. Your influence and friendship have been crucial to me.

I extend my gratitude to everyone who has worked with me over the years, enduring my mistakes and showing patience and understanding. Your support has been deeply appreciated.

Most importantly, I want to thank my Mother and Grandmother, who sacrificed greatly to raise me into the freethinker I am today. I also thank those who supported them: Johan and

Diana van Duyvendijk, Victor and Tracey Schwarz, Myra and Bill Smith, Bonnie and Scott Patrick. Your love and support have been the foundation of my success.

Thank you all for being part of this journey.

A SPECIAL OFFER FOR READERS

Earn 10 CPE/CPD credits in FloQademy!

Did you enjoy this book? Want to get CPE/CPD for reading it? Head to floqademy.floqast.com/shift-happens to earn 10 CPE/CPD in FloQademy! And while you're there, check out the many other highly entertaining, incredibly useful, and deeply informative courses we've created.

Program Description

In the ever-evolving business world, controllers need to extend their skills beyond accounting to strategic leadership. "Shift Happens: The Rise of the Operational Mindset and How Controllers Can Drive Real Value" provides key insights into the versatile controller role. Drawing experiences from top-tier finance leaders, this program offers practical advice to help controllers and accounting leaders shape their career paths.

Completion of the program requires reviewing the course materials and successfully passing the assessment with at least 70%. The assessment will expire 12 months from the registration date. Relevant topics can be found in the book's table of contents, with a glossary provided as a reference.

Learning Objectives

- Recognize the switch in the controller's role from accounting functions to strategic leadership.
- Identify how to communicate financial insights effectively to executives and partake in operational decision-making.
- Explore how an operational mindset assists controllers in merging financial knowledge with operational insights to drive value and improve organization performance.

Additional Details:

- **Recommended Prerequisites**: None
- **Delivery Method**: QAS Self Study
- **Recommended Credits**: 10
- **Field of Study**: Business Management & Organization - Non-technical
- **Program Knowledge Level**: Basic
- **Advance Preparation**: None
- **Published Date**: October 1, 2024

ABOUT THE AUTHORS

Mike Whitmire

Mike Whitmire is the CEO at FloQast, a leading Finance and Accounting Operations Platform provider, which he co-founded in 2013. As an executive, Mike puts innovation, results, and a bit of fun at the forefront of the organization. After graduating from Syracuse University with a bachelor's degree in accounting, he spent time as an auditor and accountant with experience at Ernst and Young and Cornerstone OnDemand where he helped facilitate an IPO. Outside of his roles within the accounting industry, Mike is also a published author on Amazon's Best Seller List for his book, "Controller's Code: The Secret Formula to a Successful Career in Finance." Mike's dedication to providing the best product available continues to guide FloQast while he works to address some of the outdated and less-favorable narratives that have surrounded the accounting industry for years. In his spare time, Mike enjoys woodworking and is a big baseball fan, cheering on his hometown Los Angeles Dodgers.

Stefan van Duyvendijk

Stefan is the Accounting Operations Evangelist at FloQast. Previously, Stefan served as the Corporate Controller for Kodiak Cakes, a private equity owned, leading consumer packaged food company, and as a Controller for Skullcandy, a multinational headphone CPG. These positions followed his five years at KPMG. His experience includes ASC 606 implementation, reduction of financial close timelines, accounting operational improvements, business combinations, financial statement audits, SOX audits and implementation, management reporting, debt, treasury, and systems integrations/implementation. When not evangelizing, Stefan is an avid skier and enjoys spending time on the slopes around his home in Utah.

NOTES